Daily Phonics

GRADE 3

MW00605723

Contents

Scope & Sequence

Week 1: Initial and Final Consonants
b, f, r, k, m, p, d, l, n

Week 2: Initial and Final Consonants
s, t, v, h, w, j, y, q, x, z

Week 3: Short Vowel Sounds
a, e, i, o, u

Week 4: CVC Words

Week 5: Long Vowel Sounds
a, e, i, o, u

Week 6: CVCe Words

Week 7: Syllabication

Week 8: Vowel Sounds of *y*

Week 9: Sounds of *c* and *g**

Week 10: Initial Consonant Blends
cl, fl, gl, pl, br, dr, gr*, tr, sk, sl, sp, sw, spl, str*

Week 11: Final Consonant Blends
ft, lt, nt, st, ld, nd, mp, nk

Week 12: Consonant Digraphs
ch, sh, th, wh*

Week 13: Consonant Digraphs
ph, gh, ck, ng

Week 14: Variant Spellings
dge, tch

Week 15: Silent Consonants
k, w, b, h, l

Week 16: Long Vowel Digraphs
ai, ay

Week 17: Long Vowel Digraphs
ee, ea, ey, ie

Week 18: Long Vowel Patterns
ie, igh

Week 19: Long Vowel Digraphs
oa, oe, ow

Week 20: Long Vowel Digraphs
ew, ue

Week 21: Short Vowel Digraphs
ea, ou

Week 22: The Sounds of *oo**

Week 23: Variant Vowel Digraphs
au, aw

Week 24: Diphthongs
ou, ow, oi, oy

Week 25: R-Controlled Vowels
ar, or, er, ir*, ur*

Week 26: R-Controlled Vowels
air, are*, ear**

Week 27: Plural Noun Endings
s, es, ies

Week 28: Irregular Plural Nouns

Week 29: Inflectional Verb Endings
-ed, -ing, -s, -es

Week 30: Contractions

Week 31: Prefixes
dis-, re-, un-

Week 32: Suffixes
-ful, -less, -er, -ly

*Nontransferable sound in Spanish

How to Use This Book

Daily Phonics provides systematic phonics instruction, practice, and application in a daily format. Each week focuses on one phonics skill. Daily lessons progress through scaffolded listening and speaking activities to writing and reading activities.

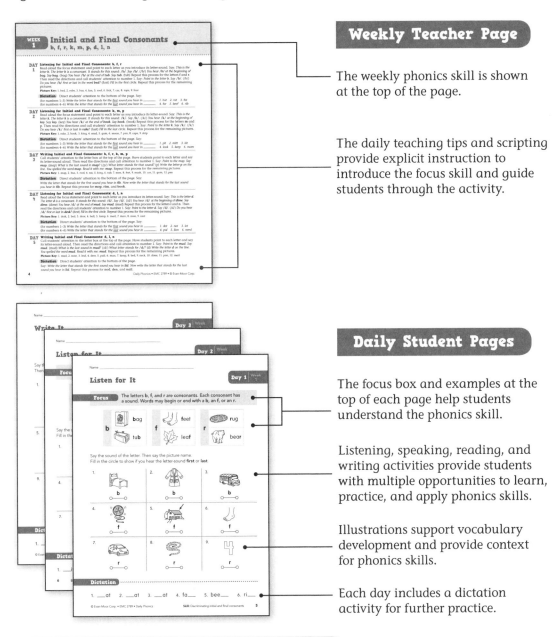

Weekly Teacher Page

The weekly phonics skill is shown at the top of the page.

The daily teaching tips and scripting provide explicit instruction to introduce the focus skill and guide students through the activity.

Daily Student Pages

The focus box and examples at the top of each page help students understand the phonics skill.

Listening, speaking, reading, and writing activities provide students with multiple opportunities to learn, practice, and apply phonics skills.

Illustrations support vocabulary development and provide context for phonics skills.

Each day includes a dictation activity for further practice.

Working with English-Language Learners

Pronunciation Is Key	Model how to pronounce letter-sounds and word chunks. Have students watch your mouth as you say a word. Then have students repeat the word.
Connect to Home Language	Be aware of nontransferable sounds and symbols in students' home languages. Help students articulate sounds in English that are new to them. Make connections to words in their home language.
Support Vocabulary Development	Develop vocabulary by connecting words to actions and providing context. Help students draw on background knowledge to connect vocabulary words to objects, concepts, actions, and situations they are familiar with.

Initial and Final Consonants
b, f, r, k, m, p, d, l, n

DAY 1

Listening for Initial and Final Consonants: b, f, r

Read aloud the focus statement and point to each letter as you introduce its letter-sound. Say: *This is the letter b. The letter b is a consonant. It stands for this sound: /b/. Say /b/.* (/b/) *You hear /b/ at the beginning of bag. Say bag.* (bag) *You hear /b/ at the end of tub. Say tub.* (tub) Repeat this process for the letters **f** and **r**. Then read the directions and call students' attention to number 1. Say: *Point to the letter b. Say /b/.* (/b/) *Do you hear /b/ first or last in the word bed?* (first) *Fill in the first circle.* Repeat this process for the remaining pictures.

Picture Key: 1. bed, 2. robe, 3. bus, 4. fan, 5. roof, 6. foot, 7. car, 8. rope, 9. four

Dictation Direct students' attention to the bottom of the page. Say:

(for numbers 1–3) *Write the letter that stands for the first sound you hear in _____.* 1. bat 2. rat 3. fat
(for numbers 4–6) *Write the letter that stands for the last sound you hear in _____.* 4. far 5. beef 6. rib

DAY 2

Listening for Initial and Final Consonants: k, m, p

Read aloud the focus statement and point to each letter as you introduce its letter-sound. Say: *This is the letter k. The letter k is a consonant. It stands for this sound: /k/. Say /k/.* (/k/) *You hear /k/ at the beginning of key. Say key.* (key) *You hear /k/ at the end of book. Say book.* (book) Repeat this process for the letters **m** and **p**. Then read the directions and call students' attention to number 1. Say: *Point to the letter k. Say /k/.* (/k/) *Do you hear /k/ first or last in rake?* (last) *Fill in the last circle.* Repeat this process for the remaining pictures.

Picture Key: 1. rake, 2. hook, 3. king, 4. mud, 5. gum, 6. moon, 7. pen, 8. cape, 9. ship

Dictation Direct students' attention to the bottom of the page. Say:

(for numbers 1–3) *Write the letter that stands for the first sound you hear in _____.* 1. pit 2. mitt 3. kit
(for numbers 4–6) *Write the letter that stands for the last sound you hear in _____.* 4. look 5. keep 6. mom

DAY 3

Writing Initial and Final Consonants: b, f, r, k, m, p

Call students' attention to the letter box at the top of the page. Have students point to each letter and say its letter-sound aloud. Then read the directions and call attention to number 1. Say: *Point to the map. Say map.* (map) *What is the last sound in map?* (/p/) *What letter stands for that sound?* (p) *Write the letter p on the line. You spelled the word map. Read it with me: map.* Repeat this process for the remaining pictures.

Picture Key: 1. map, 2. bus, 3. roof, 4. rat, 5. king, 6. tub, 7. men, 8. feet, 9. mask, 10. car, 11. gum, 12. pen

Dictation Direct students' attention to the bottom of the page. Say:

Write the letter that stands for the first sound you hear in fib. Now write the letter that stands for the last sound you hear in fib. Repeat this process for **mop**, **rim**, and **book**.

DAY 4

Listening for Initial and Final Consonants: d, l, n

Read aloud the focus statement and point to each letter as you introduce its letter-sound. Say: *This is the letter d. The letter d is a consonant. It stands for this sound: /d/. Say /d/.* (/d/) *You hear /d/ at the beginning of dime. Say dime.* (dime) *You hear /d/ at the end of mud. Say mud.* (mud) Repeat this process for the letters **l** and **n**. Then read the directions and call students' attention to number 1. Say: *Point to the letter d. Say /d/.* (/d/) *Do you hear /d/ first or last in desk?* (first) *Fill in the first circle.* Repeat this process for the remaining pictures.

Picture Key: 1. desk, 2. bed, 3. door, 4. bell, 5. lamp, 6. mail, 7. man, 8. nose, 9. nest

Dictation Direct students' attention to the bottom of the page. Say:

(for numbers 1–3) *Write the letter that stands for the first sound you hear in _____.* 1. dot 2. not 3. lot
(for numbers 4–6) *Write the letter that stands for the last sound you hear in _____.* 4. pal 5. lion 6. need

DAY 5

Writing Initial and Final Consonants: d, l, n

Call students' attention to the letter box at the top of the page. Have students point to each letter and say its letter-sound aloud. Then read the directions and call attention to number 1. Say: *Point to the mud. Say mud.* (mud) *What is the last sound in mud?* (/d/) *What letter stands for /d/?* (d) *Write the letter d on the line. You spelled the word mud. Read it with me: mud.* Repeat this process for the remaining pictures.

Picture Key: 1. mud, 2. nose, 3. leaf, 4. deer, 5. pail, 6. man, 7. lamp, 8. bed, 9. neck, 10. dime, 11. pan, 12. mail

Dictation Direct students' attention to the bottom of the page.

Say: *Write the letter that stands for the first sound you hear in lid. Now write the letter that stands for the last sound you hear in lid.* Repeat this process for **nod**, **den**, and **nail**.

Daily Phonics • EMC 2789 • © Evan-Moor Corp.

Listen for It

Focus The letters **b**, **f**, and **r** are consonants. Each consonant has a sound. Words may begin or end with a **b**, an **f**, or an **r**.

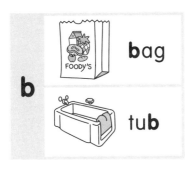

b — **b**ag / tu**b**

f — **f**eet / lea**f**

r — **r**ug / bea**r**

Say the sound of the letter. Then say the picture name.
Fill in the circle to show if you hear the letter-sound **first** or **last**.

1. **b** ○——○	2. **b** ○——○	3. **b** ○——○
4.  **f** ○——○	5.  **f** ○——○	6. **f** ○——○
7. **r** ○——○	8. **r** ○——○	9. **r** ○——○

Dictation •

1. ___at   2. ___at   3. ___at   4. fa___   5. bee___   6. ri___

Listen for It

Focus The letters **k**, **m**, and **p** are consonants. Each consonant has a sound. Words may begin or end with a **k**, an **m**, or a **p**.

k key / book

m men / farm

p pot / map

Say the sound of the letter. Then say the picture name.
Fill in the circle to show if you hear the letter-sound **first** or **last**.

1.

k
○——○

2.

k
○——○

3.

k
○——○

4.

m
○——○

5.

m
○——○

6.

m
○——○

7.

p
○——○

8.

p
○——○

9.

p
○——○

Dictation ••

1. ___it   2. ___itt   3. ___it   4. loo___   5. kee___   6. mo___

6   **Skill:** Discriminating initial and final consonants   Daily Phonics • EMC 2789 • © Evan-Moor Corp.

Name _____

Write It

Letter Box

| b | f | k | m | p | r |

Say the picture name.
Then write the letter that stands for the **first** or **last** sound you hear.

1.

ma ___

2.

___ us

3.

roo ___

4.

___ at

5.

___ ing

6.

tu ___

7.

___ en

8.

___ eet

9.

mas ___

10.

ca ___

11.

gu ___

12.

___ en

Dictation

1. ___ i ___   2. ___ o ___   3. ___ i ___   4. ___ oo ___

Skill: Writing initial and final consonants   **7**

Listen for It

Focus The letters **d**, **l**, and **n** are consonants. Each consonant has a sound. Words may begin or end with a **d**, an **l**, or an **n**.

d — **d**ime / mu**d**

l — log / nail

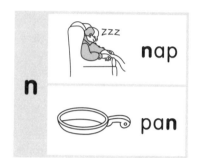

n — **n**ap / pa**n**

Say the sound of the letter. Then say the picture name.
Fill in the circle to show if you hear the letter-sound **first** or **last**.

1. **d** ○——○	2. **d** ○——○	3. **d** ○——○
4. **l** ○——○	5. **l** ○——○	6. **l** ○——○
7. **n** ○——○	8. **n** ○——○	9. **n** ○——○

Dictation ....

1. ___ot   2. ___ot   3. ___ot   4. pa___   5. lio___   6. nee___

Skill: Discriminating initial and final consonants

Write It

Letter Box

d   l   n

Say the picture name.
Then write the letter that stands for the **first** or **last** sound you hear.

1.  mu ___	2. ___ ose	3. ___ eaf	4. ___ eer
5. pai ___	6. ma ___	7. ___ amp	8. be ___
9. ___ eck	10. ___ ime	11. pa ___	12. mai ___

Dictation

1. ___i___   2. ___o___   3. ___e___   4. ___ai___

Skill: Writing initial and final consonants

Initial and Final Consonants
s, t, v, h, w, j, y, q, x, z

DAY 1 **Listening for Initial and Final Consonants: s, t, v**
Read aloud the focus statement and point to each letter as you introduce its letter-sound. Say: *This is the letter s. The letter s is a consonant. It can have this sound: /s/. Say /s/.* (/s/) *You hear /s/ at the beginning of sun. Say sun.* (sun) *You hear /s/ at the end of bus. Say bus.* (bus) Repeat the process for the letter **t**. For the letter **v**, explain that it usually comes before a silent **e** at the end of a word. Point out that for the word **five**, you only hear /v/ at the end. Explain that the **e** is silent. Then read the directions and call students' attention to number 1. Say: *Point to the letter s below the picture. Say /s/.* (/s/) *Do you hear /s/ first or last in the word sock?* (first) *Fill in the first circle.* Repeat this process for the remaining pictures.
Picture Key: 1. sock, 2. soap, 3. kiss, 4. tape, 5. boat, 6. foot, 7. wave, 8. vase, 9. cave

Dictation Direct students' attention to the bottom of the page. Say:
(for numbers 1–3) *Write the letter that stands for the <u>first</u> sound you hear in* _____. 1. top 2. vet 3. set
(for numbers 4–6) *Write the letter that stands for the <u>last</u> sound you hear in* _____. 4. vest 5. save 6. this

DAY 2 **Listening for Initial Consonants: h, w**
Read aloud the focus statement and point to each letter as you introduce its letter-sound. Say: *This is the letter h. The letter h is a consonant. It stands for this sound: /h/. Say /h/.* (/h/) *You hear /h/ at the beginning of ham. Say ham.* (ham) Repeat this process for the letter **w**. Then read the directions and call attention to number 1. Say: *Point to the worm. What is the first sound in worm?* (/w/) *What letter stands for /w/?* (w) *Circle the letter w.* Repeat this process for the remaining pictures.
Picture Key: 1. worm, 2. hand, 3. wagon, 4. wave, 5. wig, 6. hog, 7. hen, 8. hook, 9. watch

Dictation Direct students' attention to the bottom of the page. Say:
Write the letter that stands for the first sound you hear in _____. 1. hood 2. him 3. wood 4. win

DAY 3 **Listening for Initial Consonants: j, y**
Read aloud the focus statement. Then point to the letter **j** as you introduce its letter-sound. Say: *This is the letter j. The letter j is a consonant. When a word begins with j, the j usually has this sound: /j/. Say /j/.* (/j/) *You hear /j/ in jet. Say jet.* (jet) Repeat this process for the letter **y**. Then read the directions and call attention to number 1. Say: *Point to the jar. What is the first sound in jar?* (/j/) *What letter stands for /j/?* (j) *Circle the letter j.* Repeat this process for the remaining pictures.
Picture Key: 1. jar, 2. jump, 3. yawn, 4. yo-yo, 5. jacket, 6. yak, 7. yell, 8. jeans, 9. jam

Dictation Direct students' attention to the bottom of the page. Say:
Write the letter that stands for the first sound you hear in _____. 1. job 2. yet 3. just 4. yes

DAY 4 **Listening for Consonants: q, x, z**
Read aloud the focus statement. Then point to the letter **q** and say: *This is the letter q. The letter q is always followed by the letter u in a word. The letters q and u together have this sound: /kw/. Say /kw/.* (kw) *You hear /kw/ in queen. Say queen.* (queen) Then point to the letter **x** and say: *The letter x has this sound: /ks/. Say /ks/.* (ks) *You hear /ks/ at the end of fox. Say fox.* (fox) Repeat this process for **z**. Then read the directions and call students' attention to row 1. Say: *Say queen. Do you hear /kw/ in queen?* (yes) *Fill in the circle below the picture of the queen.* Repeat this process for the remaining pictures in each row.
Picture Key: Row 1: queen, vase, question mark, quilt; Row 2: box, six, jeans, fox; Row 3: kiss, zoo, zebra, zipper

Dictation Direct students' attention to the bottom of the page. Say:
(for numbers 1–3) *Write the letter that stands for the <u>first</u> sound you hear in* _____. 1. zip 2. quit 3. zebra
(for numbers 4–5) *Write the letter that stands for the <u>last</u> sound you hear in* _____. 4. fix 5. wax

DAY 5 **Writing Consonants: h, j, s, t, v, w, x, y**
Call students' attention to the letter box at the top of the page. Have students point to each letter and say its letter-sound aloud. Then read the directions and call attention to number 1. Say: *Point to the vet. What is the last sound you hear in vet?* (/t/) *What letter stands for /t/?* (t) *Write the letter t on the line. You spelled the word vet. Read it with me: vet.* Repeat this process for the remaining pictures.
Picture Key: 1. vet, 2. six, 3. jet, 4. wet, 5. hood, 6. wave, 7. hand, 8. ten, 9. jam, 10. vest, 11. nuts, 12. yak

Dictation Direct students' attention to the bottom of the page and say:
Listen to this sentence: I am in the hot sun. Write the missing letters in hot and sun.
Now listen to this sentence: The van is wet. Write the missing letters in van and wet.

Listen for It

Focus The letters **s**, **t**, and **v** are consonants. Each consonant has a sound.

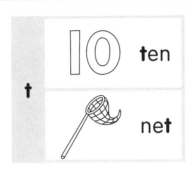

Say the sound of the letter. Then say the picture name.
Fill in the circle to show if you hear the letter-sound **first** or **last**.

1. **s** ○——○	2. **s** ○——○	3. **s** ○——○
4. **t** ○——○	5. **t** ○——○	6. 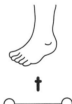 **t** ○——○
7.  **v** ○——○	8. **v** ○——○	9.  **v** ○——○

Dictation •

1. ___op   2. ___et   3. ___et   4. ves___   5. sa___e   6. thi___

Listen for It

Focus The letters **h** and **w** are consonants. Each consonant has a sound. You can usually hear **h** and **w** when they are at the beginning of words, but not when they are at the end.

 **h** ham    **w** web

Say the picture name.
Then circle the letter that stands for the **first** sound you hear.

1.
h   w

2.
h   w

3.
h   w

4.
h   w

5.
h   w

6.
h   w

7.
h   w

8.
h   w

9.
h   w

Dictation ●

1. ___ood   2. ___im   3. ___ood   4. ___in

Listen for It

Focus The letters **j** and **y** are consonants. When **j** is the first letter in a word, it usually has the sound you hear at the beginning of **jet**. When **y** is the first letter in a word, it usually has the sound you hear at the beginning of **yarn**.

 j **jet**

 y **yarn**

Say the picture name.
Then circle the letter that stands for the **first** sound you hear.

1.

j   y

2.

j   y

3.

j   y

4.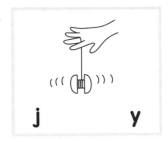

j   y

5.

j   y

6.

j   y

7.

j   y

8.

j   y

9.

j   y

Dictation •

1. ___ob   2. ___et   3. ___ust   4. ___es

Listen for It

Focus The letters **q**, **x**, and **z** are consonants. The letters **q** and **u** appear together in many words. The letter **x** is often at the end of a word. Not many words begin or end with the letter **z**.

 q **q**ueen

 x fo**x**

 z **z**ero

Say the sound that the bold letter stands for. Then say the picture name. For rows 1 and 3, fill in the circle if the picture name **begins** with that sound. For row 2, fill in the circle if the picture name **ends** with that sound.

1.

qu

○   ○   ○   ○

2.

x

○   ○   ○   ○

3.

z

○   ○   ○   ○

Dictation ··

1. ___ip   2. ___uit   3. ___ebra   4. fi___   5. wa___

Write It

Letter Box

| h | j | s | t | v | w | x | y |

Say the picture name.
Then write the letter that stands for the **first** or **last** letter-sound you hear.

1.  ve ___	2. si ___	3. ___ et	4. ___ et
5. ___ood	6.  wa ___ e	7. ___ and	8. ___ en
9. ___ am	10. ___ est	11. nut ___	12. ___ ak

Dictation ....

1. I am in the ___o___ ___u___.   2. The ___a___ is ___e___.

Skill: Writing initial and final consonants

Short Vowel Sounds
a, e, i, o, u

DAY 1

Listening for Short Vowel Sounds: a, e

Read aloud the focus statement at the top of the page. Then point to the first example as you say: *Say the word **hand**.* (hand) *Say /ă/.* (/ă/) *That is the **short a** sound.* Repeat this process for the letter **e**. Then read the directions and call students' attention to number 1. Say: *Point to the rat. Say **rat**.* (rat) *What vowel sound do you hear in **rat**?* (/ă/) *What letter stands for that sound?* (a) *Fill in the circle next to the letter **a**.* Repeat this process for the remaining pictures.

Picture Key: 1. rat, 2. web, 3. desk, 4. bag, 5. flag, 6. ten, 7. men, 8. mask, 9. stamp, 10. dress, 11. lamp, 12. neck

Dictation Direct students' attention to the bottom of the page and say:

Listen to each word I say. Then write the letter that stands for the short vowel sound you hear.
1. ran   2. pen   3. bad   4. pet   5. sad

DAY 2

Writing Short a and Short e Words

Call students' attention to the letter box at the top of the page. Have students name each vowel and say its short sound aloud. Then read the directions and call students' attention to number 1. Say: *Point to the jet. Say **jet**.* (jet) *What vowel sound do you hear in **jet**?* (/ĕ/) *What letter stands for that sound?* (e) *Write the letter **e** on the line. You spelled the word **jet**. Read it with me: **jet**.* Repeat this process for the remaining pictures.

Picture Key: 1. jet, 2. cab, 3. bed, 4. pan, 5. rat, 6. pen, 7. map, 8. yak, 9. men, 10. web, 11. nap, 12. cap

Dictation Direct students' attention to the bottom of the page and say:

Listen to each word I say. Then write the letters that stand for the sounds you hear:
1. sat   2. red   3. net   4. pad

DAY 3

Listening for Short Vowels: i, o, u

Read aloud the focus statement at the top of the page. Then point to the first example as you say: *Say the word **six**.* (six) *Say /ĭ/.* (/ĭ/) *That is the **short i** sound.* Repeat this process for the vowels **o** and **u**. Then read the directions and call students' attention to number 1. Say: *Point to the bug. Say **bug**.* (bug) *What vowel sound do you hear in **bug**?* (/ŭ/) *What letter stands for that sound?* (u) *Circle the letter **u**.* Repeat this process for the remaining pictures.

Picture Key: 1. bug, 2. rip, 3. dig, 4. fox, 5. gum, 6. mop, 7. fish, 8. sock, 9. cup, 10. pot, 11. swim, 12. cut

Dictation Direct students' attention to the bottom of the page and say:

Listen to each word I say. Then write the letter that stands for the short vowel sound you hear.
1. dip   2. box   3. run   4. pop   5. rip

DAY 4

Writing Short i, Short o, and Short u Words

Call students' attention to the letter box at the top of the page. Have students name each vowel and say its short sound aloud. Then read the directions and call students' attention to number 1. Say: *Point to the mop. Say **mop**.* (mop) *What vowel sound do you hear in **mop**?* (/ŏ/) *What letter stands for that sound?* (o) *Write the letter **o** on the line. You spelled the word **mop**. Read it with me: **mop**.* Repeat this process for the remaining pictures.

Picture Key: 1. mop, 2. cup, 3. fox, 4. lid, 5. nut, 6. six, 7. lock, 8. hill, 9. jump, 10. pot, 11. cut, 12. dig

Dictation Direct students' attention to the bottom of the page and say:

Listen to each word I say. Then write the letters that stand for the sounds you hear: *1. not   2. sit   3. rub   4. fit*

DAY 5

Reading Short Vowel Words

Read the directions and call students' attention to number 1. Say: *Let's read the incomplete sentence together: The _____ is on the _____. Now point to the words in the gray bar. Let's read them together: **lid, pan**. Which word belongs on the first line in the sentence?* (lid) *Write the word **lid** on the first line. What word should you write on the second line?* (pan) *Write **pan** on the second line.* After students have finished writing, say: *Now let's read the sentence together: **The lid is on the pan**.* Have students complete the remaining sentences independently. After students finish, guide them in reading the completed sentences.

Dictation Direct students' attention to the bottom of the page and say:

*Listen to this sentence: **Mom will sit and take a nap**. Now write the letters that stand for the sounds you hear: **mom, sit, nap**.* After students finish writing, read the sentence together.

Listen for It

Focus The letters **a** and **e** are vowels. Vowels can have a **short** sound.
You hear the **short a** sound in **hand**.
You hear the **short e** sound in **bed**.

short **a**		short **e**	
hand		bed	

Say the picture name. Listen for the **short** vowel sound.
Then fill in the circle next to the letter that stands for that sound.

1. ○ **a** ○ **e**

2. ○ **a** ○ **e**

3. ○ **a** ○ **e**

4. ○ **a** ○ **e**

5. ○ **a** ○ **e**

6. ○ **a** ○ **e**

7. ○ **a** ○ **e**

8. ○ **a** ○ **e**

9. ○ **a** ○ **e**

10. ○ **a** ○ **e**

11. ○ **a** ○ **e**

12. ○ **a** ○ **e**

Dictation •

1. r___n   2. p___n   3. b___d   4. p___t   5. s___d

Write It

Letter Box

a   e

Say the picture name. Write the letter that stands for the **short** vowel sound you hear. Then read the word.

1. j ___ t	2.  c ___ b	3. b ___ d	4. 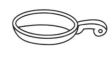 p ___ n
5. r ___ t	6. p ___ n	7. m ___ p	8. y ___ k
9. m ___ n	10. w ___ b	11. n ___ p	12. c ___ p

Dictation

1. ___ ___ ___   2. ___ ___ ___   3. ___ ___ ___   4. ___ ___ ___

Listen for It

Focus The letters **i**, **o**, and **u** are vowels. Vowels can have a **short** sound.
You hear the **short i** sound in **six**.
You hear the **short o** sound in **dot**.
You hear the **short u** sound in **tub**.

short i	6	short o	●	short u	
six		**dot**		**tub**	

Say the picture name. Listen for the **short** vowel sound.
Then circle the vowel that stands for that sound.

1.
i o u

2.
i o u

3.
i o u

4.
i o u

5.
i o u

6.
i o u

7.
i o u

8.
i o u

9.
i o u

10.
i o u

11.
i o u

12.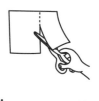
i o u

Dictation ....

1. d___p   2. b___x   3. r___n   4. p___p   5. r___p

Skill: Discriminating medial vowels   **19**

Write It

Letter Box

i   o   u

Say the picture name. Write the letter that stands for the **short** vowel sound you hear.
Then read the word.

1.  m ___ p	2. c ___ p	3.  f ___ x	4. 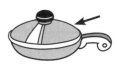 l ___ d
5. n ___ t	6. s ___ x	7. l ___ ck	8. 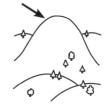 h ___ ll
9.  j ___ mp	10. p ___ t	11. c ___ t	12. d ___ g

Dictation

1. ___ ___ ___   2. ___ ___ ___   3. ___ ___ ___   4. ___ ___ ___

Daily Phonics • EMC 2789 • © Evan-Moor Corp.

Read It

Write the missing words. Then read the sentence.

1.

   lid   pan

   The _____ is on the _____.

2.

   hen   pet   Jim

   _____ has a _____ _____.

3.

   dug   nut   Sam

   _____ _____ up a _____.

4.

   can   box   top

   Put the _____ on _____ of the _____.

Dictation ....

_____ will _____ and take a _____.

CVC Words

DAY 1 — Listening for Medial Vowels

Read aloud the focus statement. Then point to the word **van** and run your finger under each letter as you say: *This word is spelled with a consonant, a vowel, and a consonant. That means the **a** in the middle has a short sound. Say **van**.* (van) *Run your finger under the letters as we read the word together: **van**.* Repeat this process for the remaining example words. Then read the directions and call students' attention to number 1. Say: *Point to the fan. Say **fan**.* (fan) *What short vowel sound do you hear in **fan**?* (/ă/) *What letter stands for that sound?* (a) *Write the letter **a** on the line to spell the word **fan**.* After students finish writing, read the word together. Repeat this process for the remaining CVC words.

Picture Key: 1. fan, 2. hot, 3. cut, 4. ten, 5. wig, 6. mop, 7. sad, 8. web, 9. hug

Dictation Direct students' attention to the bottom of the page and say:

Listen to each word I say. Then write the letters that stand for sounds you hear.
1. bun   2. tip   3. pad   4. let   5. got

DAY 2 — Listening for Medial Vowels

Read aloud the focus statement. Then point to each example, sound out the CVC word aloud, and have students repeat after you. Next, read the directions and call students' attention to number 1. Say: *Point to the pan. Say **pan**.* (pan) *Now let's read the two word choices together: **pan**, **pen**. Spell the word that goes with the picture.* (p-a-n) *Fill in the circle next to the word **pan**.* Repeat this process for the remaining pictures.

Picture Key: 1. pan, 2. bed, 3. zip, 4. mop, 5. nut, 6. men, 7. fin, 8. cab, 9. top

Dictation Direct students' attention to the bottom of the page and say:

Listen to the words I say. Then write the letters that stand for the sounds you hear.
1. get   2. not   3. run   4. mix   5. had

DAY 3 — Writing CVC Words

Call students' attention to the word box at the top of the page. Guide students in reading each word aloud. Then read the directions and call students' attention to number 1. Say: *Point to the cup. Listen to the letter-sounds in **cup**. Say **cup**.* (cup) *Find the word **cup** in the word box and write it on the line below the picture.* Repeat this process for the remaining pictures.

Picture Key: 1. cup, 2. net, 3. jam, 4. fox, 5. mat, 6. pin, 7. hen, 8. rip, 9. bus

Dictation Direct students' attention to the bottom of the page and say:

Listen to each word I say. Then write the letters that stand for the sounds you hear.
1. fat cat   2. big wig   3. hot pot

DAY 4 — Writing CVC Words

Read the directions and call students' attention to number 1. Say: *Point to the cup. What vowel sound do you hear in **cup**?* (/ŭ/) *Now let's read the word choices together: **cap**, **cup**, **cop**. Which word spells **cup**?* (c-u-p) *Circle the word **cup**, then write it on the line.* Repeat this process for the remaining rows.

Dictation Direct students' attention to the bottom of the page and say:

*Listen to this sentence: **Dad put red jam on his ham**. Now write the letters that stand for the sounds you hear: **put**, **jam**, **ham**.* After students finish writing, read the sentence together.

DAY 5 — Reading CVC Words

Read the directions and call students' attention to number 1. Say: *Let's read the incomplete sentence together: **Put the _____ in the _____**. Now, let's read the words in the gray bar together: **bag**, **can**. Which word belongs on the first line?* (can) *Write the word **can** on the line. Which word completes the sentence?* (bag) *Write the word **bag** to complete the sentence.* After students have finished writing, say: *Now let's read the sentence together: **Put the can in the bag**.* Repeat this process for the remaining sentences.

Dictation Direct students' attention to the bottom of the page and say:

*Listen to this sentence: **My pet pig can hop**. Now write the letters that stand for the sounds you hear: **pet**, **pig**, **can**, **hop**.* After students finish writing, read the sentence together.

Listen for It

Focus A vowel between two consonants has a **short** sound.

van

hen

pig

cot

nut

Say the picture name. Listen for the **short** vowel sound.
Then write the letter that stands for that sound.

1.

f ___ n

2.

h ___ t

3.

c ___ t

4.

t ___ n

5.

w ___ g

6.

m ___ p

7.

s ___ d

8.

w ___ b

9.

h ___ g

Dictation •

1. _____   2. _____   3. _____   4. _____   5. _____

Listen for It

Focus — Words that have a vowel between two consonants are called **CVC** words. The vowel in a CVC word has a **short** sound.

rat

jet

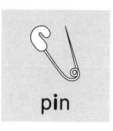
pin

fox

sun

Say the picture name. Listen for the **short** vowel sound.
Then fill in the circle next to the word that has that vowel sound.

1.
   ○ pan
   ○ pen

2.
   ○ bad
   ○ bed

3.
   ○ zap
   ○ zip

4.
   ○ mop
   ○ map

5.
   ○ net
   ○ nut

6.
   ○ man
   ○ men

7.
   ○ fan
   ○ fin

8.
   ○ cub
   ○ cab

9.
   ○ top
   ○ tip

Dictation ···

1. _____ 2. _____ 3. _____ 4. _____ 5. _____

Name _____

Write It

Word Box

mat	fox	hen
bus	rip	cup
jam	net	pin

Say the picture name. Then write the word on the line.

1.

_____

2.

_____

3.

_____

4.

_____

5.

_____

6.

_____

7.

_____

8.

_____

9.

_____

Dictation •

1. _____ _____

2. _____ _____

3. _____ _____

Skill: Writing medial vowels **25**

Write It

Say the picture name. Read the words.
Circle the word that names the picture. Then write the word on the line.

1.	cap	cup	cop	_____
2.	not	nut	net	_____
3.	fan	fun	fin	_____
4.	pet	put	pot	_____
5.	tin	ten	tan	_____
6.	pup	pep	pop	_____

Dictation

Dad _____ red _____ on his _____ .

Read It

Write the missing words. Then read the sentence.

1.

   bag   can

   Put the _____ in the _____.

2.

   map   rip

   Do not _____ the _____.

3.

   wet   mop

   The _____ is _____.

4.

   bus   dog   let

   Tim _____ the _____ onto the _____.

5.

   red   cap   sun

   My _____ has a _____ _____ on it.

Dictation

My _____ _____ _____ _____.

DAY 1

Listening for Long a and e

Read aloud the focus statement. Then point to the first example as you say: *The long sound of **a** is /ā/. Say /ā/. (/ā/) You hear /ā/ in **vase**. Say **vase**. (vase). Repeat this process for the letter **e**. Then read the directions and call students' attention to number 1. Say: Say **bee**. (bee) What long vowel sound do you hear in **bee**? (/ē/) What letter stands for that sound? (e) Circle the letter **e**. Repeat this process for the remaining pictures.*

Picture Key: 1. bee, 2. gate, 3. cake, 4. wave, 5. tree, 6. tape, 7. rake, 8. feet, 9. sheep

Dictation Direct students' attention to the bottom of the page and say:

Listen to each word I say. Then write the letter that stands for the long vowel sound you hear.
1. we   2. ape   3. he   4. same

DAY 2

Listening for Long i, o, and u

Read aloud the focus statement. Point to the first example and say: *The long sound of **i** is /ī/. Say /ī/. (/ī/) You hear /ī/ in **nine**. Say **nine**. (nine) Repeat this process for the letters **o** and **u**. Then read the directions and call students' attention to number 1. Say: Say **ice**. (ice) What long vowel sound do you hear in **ice**? (/ī/) What letter stands for that sound? (i) Circle the letter **i**. Repeat this process for the remaining pictures.*

Picture Key: 1. ice, 2. rope, 3. tube, 4. nose, 5. pie, 6. bike, 7. menu, 8. comb, 9. dime

Dictation Direct students' attention to the bottom of the page and say:

Listen to each word I say. Then write the letter that stands for the long vowel sound you hear.
1. note   2. tune   3. hike   4. robe

DAY 3

Writing Long Vowel Words

Call students' attention to the letter box at the top of the page. Have them point to each vowel and say its long sound aloud. Then read the directions and call students' attention to number 1. Point to the house and say: *This is somebody's home. Say **home**. (home) Which long vowel sound do you hear in **home**? (/ō/) What letter stands for that sound? (o) Write the letter **o** on the line. You spelled the word **home**. Run your finger under the letters as I read the word: **home**. Say **home**. (home) Repeat this process for the remaining words.*

Picture Key: 1. home, 2. cave, 3. cute, 4. me, 5. five, 6. cake, 7. tire, 8. bone, 9. mule

Dictation Direct students' attention to the bottom of the page and say:

Listen to each word I say. Then write the letter that stands for the long vowel sound you hear.
1. late   2. kite   3. we   4. note   5. use

DAY 4

Writing Long Vowel Words

Call students' attention to the letter box at the top of the page. Have them point to each vowel and say its long sound aloud. Then read the directions and call students' attention to number 1. Say: *This is a line. Say **line**. (line) Which long vowel sound do you hear in **line**? (/ī/) What letter stands for that sound? (i) Write it on the line. You spelled the word **line**. Run your finger under the letters and read with me: **line**. Repeat this process for the remaining words. For number 8, point out that many words with the long **e** sound have two **e**'s.*

Picture Key: 1. line, 2. rake, 3. mule, 4. mole, 5. pole, 6. pile, 7. wide, 8. weed, 9. wade

Dictation Direct students' attention to the bottom of the page and say:

Listen to each word I say. Then write the letter that stands for the long vowel sound you hear.
1. bike   2. home   3. tube   4. same   5. week

DAY 5

Reviewing Long and Short Vowel Sounds

Read the directions and call students' attention to row 1. Say: *What long vowel sound does the letter **a** stand for? (/ā/) Point to the cage. Do you hear /ā/ in **cage**? (yes) Circle the picture of the cage. Repeat this process for the remaining pictures in each row. If you wish, have students name each picture.*

Picture Key: Row 1: cage, rat, bag, vase; Row 2: web, vest, tree, zebra; Row 3: fin, tire, nine, bib; Row 4: comb, mop, pot, nose; Row 5: nuts, menu, tube, cup

Dictation Direct students' attention to the bottom of the page and say:

Listen to each sentence. Then write the missing letters that stand for the long vowel sounds you hear.
1. Wave to the mule.   2. Hide the bone.

Listen for It

Focus A vowel can have a **long** sound. The long sound says the vowel's name. You hear the **long a** sound in **vase**. You hear the **long e** sound in **me**.

long **a**		long **e**	
v**a**se		m**e**	

Say the picture name. Listen to the **long** vowel sound.
Then circle the vowel that stands for that sound.

1.

a   e

2.

a   e

3.

a   e

4.

a   e

5.

a   e

6.

a   e

7.

a   e

8.

a   e

9.

a   e

Dictation

1. w___   2. ___pe   3. h___   4. s___me

Listen for It

Focus A vowel can have a **long** sound. The long sound says the vowel's name. You hear the **long i** sound in **nine**. You hear the **long o** sound in **bone**. You hear the **long u** sound in **cube**.

long **i** nine	9	long **o** bone		long **u** cube	

Say the picture name. Listen to the **long** vowel sound.
Then circle the letter that stands for that sound.

1.

   i   o   u

2.

   i   o   u

3.

   i   o   u

4.

   i   o   u

5.

   i   o   u

6.

   i   o   u

7.

   i   o   u

8.

   i   o   u

9.

   i   o   u

Dictation •

1. n___te   2. t___ne   3. h___ke   4. r___be

Write It

Letter Box

a	e	i	o	u

Say the picture name.
Then write the letter that stands for the **long** vowel sound you hear.

1.  h ___ me	2.  c ___ ve	3.  c ___ te
4.  m ___	5. f ___ ve	6. c ___ ke
7. t ___ re	8. b ___ ne	9. m ___ le

Dictation

1. l___te   2. k___te   3. w___   4. n___te   5. ___se

Skill: Writing words with long vowels   **31**

Name _____

Write It

Letter Box

a   e   i   o   u

Say the picture name. Listen to the **long** vowel sound.
Then write the letter that stands for that sound.

1. ———— l ___ ne	2. r ___ ke	3.  m ___ le
4. m ___ le	5. p ___ le	6.  p ___ le
7. w ___ de	8.  w ___ ed	9. w ___ de

Dictation ●

1. b ___ ke   2. h ___ me   3. t ___ be   4. s ___ me   5. w ___ ek

Review It

Say the picture name.
Circle the picture when you hear a **long** vowel sound.
Underline the picture when you hear a **short** vowel sound.

1.	**a**				
2.	**e**				
3.	**i**				
4.	**o**				
5.	**u**				

Dictation

1. W___ve to the m___le.   2. H___de the b___ne.

Skill: Discriminating short and long vowel sounds

DAY 1

Reading CVCe Words

Read aloud the focus statement. Then point to the example as you explain the CVCe pattern. Say: *This word says kit. It is a CVC word. The vowel in a CVC word is short. When we add a silent e to the word kit, it becomes the word kite. Now it is a CVCe word. The final e is silent, but it makes the letter i have the long i sound.* Then read the directions and call students' attention to number 1. Say: *Let's read this word together: tub. Now write the final e on the line. Let's read the new word: tube. The u has a long sound. The final e is not sounded. Point to the picture that shows a tube. Fill in the circle under the tube.* Repeat this process for the remaining words. **Picture Key:** 1. tube, 2. mane, 3. robe, 4. tape, 5. pine, 6. pane

Dictation Direct students' attention to the bottom of the page and say:

Listen to each word I say. Then write the letters that stand for the sounds you hear.
1. rat, rate   2. hop, hope

DAY 2

Reading CVCe Words

Read aloud the focus statement. Read the directions and call students' attention to number 1. Say: *This picture shows tape. Say tape. (tape) What long vowel sound do you hear in tape? (long a; /ā/) Write the letter a on the first line. Now we need to write a silent e on the last line to make the a have a long vowel sound. Let's read the word together: tape.* Repeat this process for the remaining words.

Picture Key: 1. tape, 2. kite, 3. bike, 4. rope, 5. pipe, 6. name, 7. tube, 8. frame, 9. smoke

Dictation Direct students' attention to the bottom of the page and say:

Listen to each word I say. Then write the vowel you hear and a final silent e to spell the word.
1. tame   2. ride   3. note   4. tune

DAY 3

Writing CVCe Words

Call students' attention to the word box at the top of the page. Have students read each word aloud. Then read the directions and call students' attention to number 1. Say: *This is a pine tree. Say pine. (pine) Find the word pine in the word box. How is pine spelled? (p-i-n-e) Write the word pine on the lines.* Repeat this process for the remaining pictures.

Picture Key: 1. pine, 2. mule, 3. hole, 4. rope, 5. hide, 6. rake

Dictation Direct students' attention to the bottom of the page and say:

Listen to each word I say. Then write the letters that stand for the sounds you hear.
1. mine   2. tube   3. bake   4. poke

DAY 4

Writing CVCe Words

Read the directions and call students' attention to number 1. Say: *Point to the rope. Say rope. (rope) What vowel sound do you hear in rope? (/ō/) Now let's read the word choices together: rope, ripe. Which word spells rope? (r-o-p-e) Circle the word rope, then write it on the line.* Repeat this process for the remaining pictures.

Picture Key: 1. rope, 2. bike, 3. dime, 4. tube, 5. pole, 6. lane, 7. mole, 8. mane

Dictation Direct students' attention to the bottom of the page and say:

Listen to each word I say. Then write the letters that stand for the sounds you hear.
1. lime   2. time   3. name   4. home

DAY 5

Reading CVCe Words

Read the directions and call students' attention to number 1. Say: *This picture shows a cone that grows on a pine tree. Two words are missing in the sentence. Let's read the incomplete sentence together: A _____ _____ has seeds. Now point to the words in the gray bar. Let's read them together: cone, pine. Which word belongs on the first line in the sentence? (pine) Write the word pine on the line. Which word completes the sentence? (cone)* After students have finished writing, say: *Now let's read the sentence together: A pine cone has seeds.* Repeat this process for the remaining sentences.

Dictation Direct students' attention to the bottom of the page and say:

Listen to this sentence: Tom will tape the kite. Now write the missing words: tape, kite. After students finish writing, read the sentence together.

Read It

Focus Some words have a CVCe pattern. The vowel in the middle has a **long** sound. The **e** at the end is silent.

 kit + e = kite

Read the word. Add a final **e** to make a new word.
Then fill in the circle under the picture that matches the new word.

1.

tub___

○   ○

2.

man___

○   ○

3.

rob___

○   ○

4.

tap___

○   ○

5.

pin___

○   ○

6.

pan___

○   ○

Dictation ●

1. _____ _____   2. _____ _____

Read It

Focus The vowel in the middle of a CVCe word has a **long** sound. The final **e** is silent.

Letter Box

| a | e | i | o | u |

Say the picture name.
Write the letter that stands for the **long** vowel sound.
Then write the silent **e** at the end of the word.

1. t __ p __	2. k __ t __	3. b __ k __
4. r __ p __	5. p __ p __	6. n __ m __
7. t __ b __	8. fr __ m __	9. sm __ k __

Dictation •

1. t __ m __   2. r __ d __   3. n __ t __   4. t __ n __

Write It

Word Box

hid	hide	hole	pine
rake	mule	pin	rope

Say the picture name. Then write the word on the lines.
You will use only six of the words in the box.

1. ___ ___ ___ ___

2. ___ ___ ___ ___

3. ___ ___ ___ ___

4. ___ ___ ___ ___

5. ___ ___ ___ ___

6. ___ ___ ___ ___

Dictation

1. _____ 2. _____ 3. _____ 4. _____

Write It

Say the picture name. Read the words.
Circle the word that names the picture. Then write the word on the line.

1.		rope	ripe	_____
2.		bake	bike	_____
3.		dome	dime	_____
4.		tune	tube	_____
5.		pole	pile	_____
6.		lone	lane	_____
7.		mile	mole	_____
8.		mane	mine	_____

Dictation

1. _____   2. _____   3. _____   4. _____

Read It

Write the missing words. Then read the sentence.

1.

   cone   pine

   A _____ _____ has seeds.

2.

   mole   hole

   A _____ can dig a _____.

3.

   name   same

   Mom and I have the _____ _____.

4.

   bikes   rule

   What is the _____ about _____?

5.

   mule   ride   safe

   It is _____ to _____ that _____.

Dictation •

Tom will _____ the _____.

Syllabication

DAY 1

Counting Syllables

Read aloud the focus statement. Point to the first example and say: *Listen to this word: gate. Say gate.* (gate) *How many vowel sounds do you hear in gate?* (1—/ā/) *The word gate has one vowel sound, so it has one syllable.* Repeat this process for **napkin**. Then read the directions and call students' attention to number 1. Say: *The picture shows a bone. Say bone.* (bone) *How many vowel sounds do you hear in bone?* (1) *Write the number 1 in the first box. How many syllables do you hear in bone?* (1) *Write the number 1 in the next box.* Repeat this process for the remaining words.

Picture Key: 1. bone, 2. menu, 3. penny, 4. elephant, 5. lamp, 6. banana

Dictation   Direct students' attention to the bottom of the page and say:

Listen to each word I say. Then write the letters that stand for the sounds you hear. Write the number of syllables in the box.   *1. pen   2. sunset   3. napkin*

DAY 2

Dividing Words into Syllables

Read aloud the focus statement. Point to the first example and say: *Listen to this word: magnet. Say magnet.* (magnet) *Which two consonants are in the middle of this word?* (g, n) *Trace the line to divide the word into syllables. Point to each syllable as you read the word: mag·net.* Repeat this process for **tennis**. Then read the directions and call students' attention to number 1. Say: *Say rabbit.* (rabbit) *What are the two middle consonants?* (b, b) *Draw a line to divide the word into syllables. Let's read each syllable together: rab·bit.* Repeat this process for the remaining words.

Dictation   Direct students' attention to the bottom of the page and say:

Listen to each word I say. Then write the letters that stand for the sounds you hear. Write the number of syllables in the box.   *1. dive   2. inside   3. upset*

DAY 3

Reading Two-Syllable Words

Read aloud the focus statement. Point to the word **muffin** and say: *This word is divided into two syllables. Look at the first syllable. Is it a closed syllable?* (yes) *How do you know it's closed?* (It ends in a consonant. It ends with the letter **f**.) *Will the **u** have a short or long sound?* (short) *Now look at the second syllable. Is it a closed syllable?* (yes) *How do you know?* (It ends in a consonant. It ends with the letter **n**.) *Will the **i** have a short or long sound?* (short) *Let's read the word together: muffin.* Then read the directions and call attention to number 1. Say: *Look at the first syllable in the word. Is it a closed syllable?* (yes) *Will the **u** have a short sound?* (yes) *Underline the **u**. Now point to the second syllable in the word. Is it a closed syllable?* (yes) *Will the **i** have a short sound?* (yes) *Underline the **i**. Now let's read the word together: pumpkin.* Repeat this process for the remaining words. Guide students in identifying the long vowels in numbers 2 through 6.

Dictation   Direct students' attention to the bottom of the page and say:
Listen to each word I say. Then write the word on the line.   *1. bedtime   2. rabbit*

DAY 4

Reading Two-Syllable Words

Read aloud the focus statement. Point to the first syllable in the word **robot** and ask: *Is this an open syllable?* (yes) *How do you know?* (It ends in a vowel.) *Will the **o** have a short or a long sound?* (long) Point to the last syllable and ask: *Is this an open or closed syllable?* (closed) *What sound will the **o** have?* (short) Then read the directions and call attention to number 1. Say: *Point to the first syllable in the word.* (hu) *Is it an open or closed syllable?* (open) *How do you know it's an open syllable?* (It ends in a vowel.) *Will the **u** have a short or a long sound?* (long) *Underline the **u**. Let's read the word: human.* Repeat this process for the remaining words, applying the open or closed syllable rule to read each word.

Dictation   Direct students' attention to the bottom of the page and say:
Listen to each word I say. Then write the word on the line.   *1. menu   2. hotel*

DAY 5

Reading Two-Syllable Words

Read the directions and call students' attention to number 1. Say: *Point to the first word. The first syllable is underlined. Is the syllable open or closed?* (open) *How do you know?* (The syllable ends in a vowel—a) *Make a check in the box under open syllable. Will the letter **a** have a short or long sound?* (long) *Make a check in the box under long vowel. Now let's read the word together: bacon.* Repeat this process for the remaining words.

Dictation   Direct students' attention to the bottom of the page and say:
Listen to this sentence: Put the bacon in the basket. Write the words on the line.

Listen for It

Focus A syllable is a word part that has one vowel sound.
A word can have more than one syllable.

 gate
1 vowel sound = **1** syllable

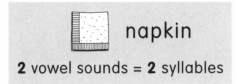 napkin
2 vowel sounds = **2** syllables

Say each picture name. Listen for the vowel sounds. Write how many vowel sounds you hear. Then write how many syllables the word has.

	vowel sounds	syllables
1.		
2.		
3.		
4.		
5.		
6.		

Dictation •

1. _____ ☐   2. _____ ☐   3. _____ ☐

Listen for It

Focus Many words have two syllables. The first syllable ends with a consonant. The second syllable begins with a consonant. Both syllables have a vowel sound.

mag·net

ten·nis

Say the picture name.
Then draw a line to divide the word into syllables.

1. rabbit	2. button	3. napkin
4. basket	5. muffin	6. sunset
7. puppet	8. letter	9. pretzel

Dictation ··

1. _____ ☐ 2. _____ ☐ 3. _____ ☐

Name _____

Read It

Focus A syllable that ends in a consonant is called a **closed** syllable. The vowels in a closed syllable usually have a **short** sound.

muf·fin

Look at the syllables in the word. Underline the vowel or vowels that have a **short** sound. Then blend the syllables to read the word.

1.	2.	3.
pump•kin	pen•ny	ro•bot
4.	5.	6.
ho•tel	pup•py	men•u
7.	8.	9.
up•set	nap•kin	lim•it

Dictation ●●

1. _____   2. _____

Skill: Dividing two-syllable words   **43**

Read It

Focus A syllable that ends in a vowel is called an **open** syllable. The first vowel in an open syllable usually has a **long** sound.

ro:bot

Look at the syllables in the word. Underline the vowel that has a **long** sound. Then read the word out loud.

1. hu•man	2. tu•lip	3. ba•by
4. $\begin{array}{r} 4 \\ -2 \\ \hline 2 \end{array}$ mi•nus	5. la•dy	6. pi•lot
7. yo•yo	8. mu•sic	9. o•pen

Dictation •••

1. _____   2. _____

Read It

Look at the syllable that is underlined in each word. Read the word out loud. Then check the correct boxes. The first one has been done for you.

	closed syllable	open syllable	short vowel	long vowel
1. <u>ba</u>con		✓		✓
2. <u>rot</u>ten				
3. <u>pen</u>ny				
4. rab<u>bit</u>				
5. hell<u>o</u>				
6. <u>pu</u>pil				
7. ro<u>bot</u>				
8. <u>ze</u>bra				

Dictation ••

_____

DAY 1

Listening for Long i and Long e

Read aloud the focus statement. Then point to the first example as you say: *The word **sky** ends in the consonant **k** and the letter **y**. Say **sky**.* (sky) *You hear the **long i** sound at the end of **sky**.* Then point to the word **penny** and say: *The word **penny** ends in the consonant **n** and the letter **y**. Say **penny**.* (penny) *You can hear the **long e** sound at the end of **penny**.* Then read the directions and call students' attention to number 1. Say: *Point to the girl who is crying. Say **cry**.* (cry) *What sound does the **y** have?* (long i; /ī/) *Circle **long i**.* Repeat this process for the remaining words.

Dictation Direct students' attention to the bottom of the page and say:

*Listen to each word I say. Then write the word you hear. Each word ends with the letter **y**.*
1. cry 2. dry 3. penny

DAY 2

Listening for Long i and Long e

Read aloud the focus statement. Then point to the first example and say: *Say **sky**.* (sky) *How many syllables does **sky** have?* (one) *What vowel sound do you hear in **sky**?* (/ī/) Point to the second example and say: *Say **penny**.* (penny) *How many syllables does **penny** have?* (two) *What two vowel sounds do you hear in **penny**?* (/ĕ/, /ē/) Then read the directions and call students' attention to number 1. Say: *Run your finger under the letters as we read this word together: **sunny**. What vowel sounds do you hear in **sunny**?* (/ŭ/, /ē/) *How many syllables are in **sunny**?* (two) *Fill in the circle next to the number 2. What sound does the **y** in **sunny** have?* (/ē/) *Fill in the circle next to the letter **e**.* Repeat this process for the remaining words.

Dictation Direct students' attention to the bottom of the page and say:

*Listen to each word I say. Then write the word you hear. Each word ends with the letter **y**.*
1. puppy 2. fly 3. lady

DAY 3

Writing Words That End in y

Read the directions and call students' attention to the word box. Say: *Point to the first word and read it with me: **fly**. Does the letter **y** have a **long i** sound or a **long e** sound in **fly**?* (long i) *Write the word **fly** on the line in the box that says **y = long i**.* Repeat this process for the remaining words.

Dictation Direct students' attention to the bottom of the page and say:

Listen to each word I say. Then write the word you hear.   *1. spy 2. sunny 3. penny*

DAY 4

Reviewing Words That End in y

Read aloud the directions. Then point to the picture in row 1. Say: *This picture shows a spy. Say **spy**.* (spy) *Read the words in this row and circle the word that spells **spy**.* After students circle a word, ask: *Which word did you circle? Spell it.* (s-p-y) Repeat this process for the remaining pictures.

Picture Key: 1. spy, 2. lady, 3. fry, 4. pony, 5. sunny, 6. fly, 7. puppy, 8. sky

Dictation Direct students' attention to the bottom of the page and say:

*Listen to this sentence: **The lady is a spy**. Write the words on the line.*

DAY 5

Reading Words That End in y

Read aloud the directions and call students' attention to number 1. Say: *This picture shows a smiling baby. Two words are missing in the sentence. Let's read the incomplete sentence together: **The cute _____ is _____**. Now point to the two words in the gray bar. Let's read them together: **baby, happy**. Which word belongs on the first line in the sentence?* (baby) *Write **baby** on the line. Which word should you write on the second line?* (happy) After students finish writing, say: *Now let's read the sentence together: **The cute baby is happy**.* Repeat this process for the remaining sentences.

Dictation Direct students' attention to the bottom of the page and say:

*Listen to this sentence: **The baby will cry**. Write the words on the line.*

Listen for It

Focus When a word ends with a consonant + **y**, the **y** has a vowel sound. The **y** has a **long i** or **long e** sound.

y = long i sky		y = long e penny	

Say the picture name. Then read the word. Listen to the sound of **y**.
Circle **long i** or **long e** to show which long vowel sound you hear.

1.
cry
long i   long e

2.
puppy
long i   long e

3.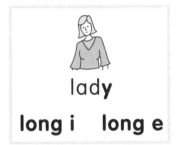
lady
long i   long e

4.
spy
long i   long e

5.
fry
long i   long e

6.
baby
long i   long e

7.
pony
long i   long e

8.
fly
long i   long e

9.
bunny
long i   long e

Dictation •

1. _____   2. _____   3. _____

Listen for It

Focus A **y** usually has the **long i** sound in words that have one syllable.
A **y** usually has the **long e** sound in words that have two syllables.

sky		1
long **i**		syllable

penny		2
long **e**		syllables

Say the word. How many syllables do you hear?
Fill in the circle next to that number.
Then fill in the circle next to **i** or **e** to show what sound the **y** has.

1.
sunny

syllables	sound
○ **1**	○ **i**
○ **2**	○ **e**

2.
bunny

syllables	sound
○ **1**	○ **i**
○ **2**	○ **e**

3.
spy

syllables	sound
○ **1**	○ **i**
○ **2**	○ **e**

4.
pony

syllables	sound
○ **1**	○ **i**
○ **2**	○ **e**

5.
cry

syllables	sound
○ **1**	○ **i**
○ **2**	○ **e**

6.
fry

syllables	sound
○ **1**	○ **i**
○ **2**	○ **e**

Dictation ....

1. _____ 2. _____ 3. _____

Write It

Word Box

fly	happy	my	funny	fry
sky	pony	baby	cry	puppy

Read the word. Do you hear **long i** or **long e**?
Write the word in the correct box.

y = long i	**y = long e**
_____	_____
_____	_____
_____	_____
_____	_____
_____	_____

Dictation

1. _____   2. _____   3. _____

Review It

Say the picture name. Then read the words.
Circle the word that names the picture.

1.	sixty	sky	spy
2.	lady	baby	daddy
3.	sly	try	fry
4.	puppy	pony	penny
5.	sunny	funny	silly
6.	try	fry	fly
7.	penny	puppy	pony
8.	spy	sly	sky

Dictation

• •

_____

Read It

Write the missing words. Then read the sentence.

1.

baby   happy

The cute _____ is _____.

2.

spy   funny

Is that _____ man a _____?

3.

pony   try

I will _____ to ride a _____.

4.

fly   sky

The kite will _____ in the _____.

5.

puppy   lady   my

Did the _____ see _____ _____?

Dictation •

_____

Sounds of c and g

DAY 1
Listening for Hard c

Read aloud the focus statement. Then point to each example as you introduce the hard sound of **c**. Say: *The hard sound of **c** has the same sound as the letter **k**: /k/. Say /k/. (/k/) You hear /k/ in **cat, cot,** and **cup**.* Have students point to each example word and read it. Then read aloud the directions and call students' attention to number 1. Say: *Look at the word. What letter follows the **c** in this word? (a) Will this **c** have a hard sound? (yes) Let's read the word together: **cake**. Does **cake** have the (/k/) sound? (yes) Fill in the circle next to **yes**.* Repeat this process for the remaining words.

Dictation Direct students' attention to the bottom of the page and say:

*Each word I am going to say begins with the letter **c**. Listen to each word I say. Then write the word you hear.*
1. cape   2. cone   3. cut

DAY 2
Listening for Soft c

Read aloud the focus statement. Then point to each example as you introduce the soft sound of **c**. Say: *The soft sound of **c** has the same sound as the letter **s**: /s/. Say /s/. (/s/) You hear /s/ in **face** and **city**.* Have students point to each example word and read it. Then read aloud the directions and call students' attention to number 1. Say: *Look at the word. What letter follows **c** in this word? (e) According to the rule, does this **c** have a soft sound? (yes) Let's read the word together: **cent**. Does the word **cent** have the **soft c** sound? (yes) Fill in the circle next to the word **yes**.* Repeat this process for the remaining words.

Dictation Direct students' attention to the bottom of the page and say:

*Each word I am going to say has the letter **c** in it. Listen to each word I say. Then write the word you hear.*
1. face   2. race   3. pencil

DAY 3
Listening for Hard g

Read aloud the focus statement. Then point to each example as you introduce the hard sound of **g**. Say: *You hear /g/ in **gas**. Say **gas**. (gas) Say /g/. (/g/) Repeat this process for **gold, gum,** and **frog**.* Then read aloud the directions and call students' attention to number 1. Say: *Look at the word. What letter follows the **g** in this word? (e) According to the rule, this **g** will not have the hard sound. Let's read the word: **gem**. Do you hear the sound of **hard g** in **gem**? (no) Fill in the circle next to **no**. Point to number 2. Look at the word. What letter follows the **g** in this word? (no letter; g is the last letter) According to the rule, this **g** will have the hard sound. Let's read the word together: **bug**. Do you hear the sound of **hard g** in **bug**? (yes) Fill in the circle next to **yes**.* Repeat this process for the remaining words.

Dictation Direct students' attention to the bottom of the page and say:

Listen to each word I say. Then write the word you hear.   1. got   2. gut   3. gap   4. sag

DAY 4
Listening for Soft g

Read aloud the focus statement. Then point to each example word as you introduce the soft sound of **g**. Say: *The letter **g** can have the same sound as the letter **j**: /j/. Say /j/. (/j/) You hear /j/ in **gem** and **giant**.* Have students point to each example word and read it. Then read aloud the directions and call students' attention to number 1. Say: *What letter follows the **g** in this word? (u) According to the rule, will this **g** have the sound of /j/? (no) Let's read the word together: **gum**. Do you hear the sound of **soft g** in **gum**? (no) Fill in the circle next to the word **no**.* Repeat this process for the remaining words.

Dictation Direct students' attention to the bottom of the page and say:

*Each word I am going to say has the letter **g** in it. Listen to each word. Then write the word you hear.*
1. gel   2. age

DAY 5
Reading Words with c and/or g

Read aloud the directions and then call students' attention to number 1. Say: *The first picture shows a stick of gum. Say **gum**. (gum) Write the missing letter to spell the word **gum**. The next picture shows a penny. A penny can be called a **cent**. Say **cent**. (cent) Write the missing letter to spell the word **cent**. Now let's read the incomplete sentence together: **The _____ costs one _____.** Which word belongs on the first line? (gum) Write the word **gum**. What word should you write on the second line? (cent)* After students finish writing, say: *Now let's read the sentence together: **The gum costs one cent**.* Repeat this process for the remaining sentences.

Dictation Direct students' attention to the bottom of the page and say:

*Listen to this sentence: **I have gum on my face!** Write the missing words on the lines.*

Listen for It

Focus The letter **c** can have the **hard** sound of **/k/** or the **soft** sound of **/s/**. The letter **c** usually has the **/k/** sound when it is followed by an **a**, an **o**, or a **u**.

c = /k/ sound

cat   **co**t   **cu**p

Look at the word. Does the **c** have the **/k/** sound?
Fill in the circle next to **yes** or **no**.

1.

cake

○ yes   ○ no

2.

can

○ yes   ○ no

3.

ice

○ yes   ○ no

4.

corn

○ yes   ○ no

5.

face

○ yes   ○ no

6.

cube

○ yes   ○ no

Dictation ∙∙

1. _____   2. _____   3. _____

Listen for It

Focus The letter **c** can have the **hard** sound of /k/ or the **soft** sound of /s/. The letter **c** usually has the /s/ sound when it is followed by an **e** or an **i**.

c = /s/ sound

fa**ce**   **ci**ty

Look at the word. Does the **c** have the /s/ sound?
Fill in the circle next to **yes** or **no**.

1.	2.	3.
cent	cane	rice
○ yes ○ no	○ yes ○ no	○ yes ○ no

4.	5.	6.
cub	fence	pencil
○ yes ○ no	○ yes ○ no	○ yes ○ no

Dictation ....

1. _____   2. _____   3. _____

Listen for It

Focus

The letter **g** can have the **hard** sound of /g/ or the **soft** sound of /j/. The letter **g** usually has the /g/ sound when it is followed by an **a**, an **o**, or a **u**, or when it is the last letter of a word.

g = /g/ sound

 gas

 gold

 gum

 fro**g**

Look at the word. Does the **g** have the **/g/** sound?
Fill in the circle next to **yes** or **no**.

1.

gem

○ yes   ○ no

2.

bug

○ yes   ○ no

3.

orange

○ yes   ○ no

4.

gate

○ yes   ○ no

5.

wagon

○ yes   ○ no

6.

gull

○ yes   ○ no

Dictation •

1. _____   2. _____   3. _____   4. _____

Skill: Listening for the **hard** sound of g

Listen for It

Focus The letter **g** can have the **hard** sound of /g/ or the **soft** sound of /j/. The letter **g** usually has the /j/ sound when it is followed by an **e** or an **i**.

g = /j/ sound

gem

giant

Look at the word. Does the **g** have the /j/ sound?
Fill in the circle next to **yes** or **no**.

1.  gum ○ yes ○ no	2. cage ○ yes ○ no	3.  golf ○ yes ○ no
4.  page ○ yes ○ no	5.  magic ○ yes ○ no	6.  gas ○ yes ○ no

Dictation ···

1. ___el   2. a___e

Read It

Say the picture name. Write a **c** or a **g** to spell the word.
Then write the words to complete the sentence. Read the sentence out loud.

1. ___um   ___ent

   The _____ costs one _____.

2.  wa___on   fla___

   Put the _____ in the _____.

3. ___age   mi___e

   The _____ ran inside a large _____.

4. ___ave   ___iant

   Does a _____ sleep in this _____?

5. hu___e   ___ate

   The mice cannot open the _____ _____.

Dictation ••

I have _____ on my _____!

Initial Consonant Blends
cl, fl, gl, pl, br, dr, gr, tr, sk, sl, sp, sw, spl, str

DAY 1

Listening for Initial Blends: cl, fl, gl, pl
Read aloud the focus statement. Then point to the first example and say: *The letters c and l blend together to make this sound: /kl/. Say /kl/.* (/kl/) *You hear /kl/ in the word club. Say club.* (club) Repeat this process for the remaining examples. Then read the directions and call attention to number 1. Say: *Point to the plug. Say plug.* (plug) *What blend do you hear at the beginning of plug?* (/pl/) *Which letters stand for that sound?* (pl) *Fill in the circle next to the letters pl.* Repeat this process for the remaining pictures.
Picture Key: 1. plug, 2. flag, 3. globe, 4. cliff, 5. clam, 6. plant, 7. flame, 8. glue, 9. planet

Dictation Direct students' attention to the bottom of the page and say:
Listen to each word I say. Then write the word you hear. 1. *flip* 2. *clip* 3. *plan*

DAY 2

Listening for Initial Blends: br, dr, gr, tr
Read aloud the focus statement. Then point to the first example and say: *The letters b and r blend together to make this sound: /br/. Say /br/.* (/br/) *You hear /br/ in the word brave. Say brave.* (brave) Repeat this process for the remaining examples. Then read the directions and call attention to number 1. Say: *Point to the tree. Say tree.* (tree) *What blend do you hear at the beginning of tree?* (/tr/) *Which letters stand for that sound?* (tr) *Fill in the circle next to the letters tr.* Repeat this process for the remaining pictures.
Picture Key: 1. tree, 2. brick, 3. grapes, 4. grill, 5. drum, 6. bride, 7. dress, 8. trash, 9. dragon

Dictation Direct students' attention to the bottom of the page and say:
Listen to each word I say. Then write the word you hear. 1. *drip* 2. *grip* 3. *broke*

DAY 3

Reading Words with Initial Blends: cl, fl, gl, pl, br, dr, gr, tr
Read aloud the first set of directions and call students' attention to number 1. Say: *What does the first picture show?* (a tree) *What blend do you hear at the beginning of tree?* (/tr/) *Which letters have that sound?* (tr) *Write tr on the lines. Now let's read the word: tree.* Repeat this process for the remaining pictures. Then read aloud the directions for the second activity. Call students' attention to number 1 and say: *The picture shows hands clapping. Now let's read the incomplete sentence together: Will you _____ when I do a _____? Now let's read the words in the gray bar: clap, flap, flip. Which words complete the sentence?* (clap, flip) *Write the words on the lines. Now let's read the sentence together: Will you clap when I do a flip?* Have students complete the next sentence independently.

Dictation Direct students' attention to the bottom of the page and say:
Listen to this sentence: Do not drop the brick. Write the words on the line.

DAY 4

Listening for Initial Blends: sk, sl, sp, sw, spl, str
Read aloud the focus statement. Then point to the first example and say: *The letters s and k blend together to make this sound: /sk/. Say /sk/.* (/sk/) *You hear /sk/ in the word skip. Say skip.* (skip) Repeat this process for the remaining examples and point out that the blends spl and str have three blended sounds. Then read the directions and call attention to number 1. Say: *Point to the sled. Say sled.* (sled) *What blend do you hear at the beginning of sled?* (/sl/) *Which letters stand for that sound?* (sl) *Fill in the circle next to the letters sl.* Repeat this process for the remaining pictures.
Picture Key: 1. sled, 2. swim, 3. sleep, 4. skate, 5. swan, 6. space, 7. skunk, 8. street, 9. splash

Dictation Direct students' attention to the bottom of the page and say:
Listen to each word I say. Then write the word you hear. 1. *slip* 2. *spot* 3. *skin* 4. *strap*

DAY 5

Reading Words with Initial Blends: sk, sl, sp, sw, spl, str
Read aloud the first set of directions and call students' attention to number 1. Say: *What does the first picture show?* (a skate) *Which blend do you hear at the beginning of skate?* (sk) *Which letters have that sound?* (sk) *Write sk on the lines. Now let's read the word together: skate.* Repeat this process for the remaining pictures. Then read aloud the directions for the second activity. Call students' attention to number 1 and say: *The picture shows a girl swimming. Now let's read the incomplete sentence together: Stella can _____ and _____. Now let's read the words in the gray bar together: slim, splash, swim. Which words complete the sentence?* (swim, splash) *Write the words on the lines. Now let's read the sentence together: Stella can swim and splash.* Have students complete the next sentence independently.

Dictation Direct students' attention to the bottom of the page and say:
Listen to this sentence: Do not skate in the street. Write the words on the line.

Name _____

Listen for It

| **Focus** | Two consonant sounds said together are called a **consonant blend**. Many words begin with a **consonant + l** blend. |

| **cl** club | **fl** flip | **gl** glad | **pl** plot |

Say the picture name.
Then fill in the circle next to the blend you hear at the **beginning**.

1. ○ cl ○ fl ○ pl

2. ○ cl ○ fl ○ pl

3. ○ gl ○ pl ○ fl

4. ○ cl ○ fl ○ pl

5. ○ cl ○ fl ○ pl

6. ○ gl ○ pl ○ fl

7.  ○ cl ○ fl ○ pl

8. ○ gl ○ pl ○ fl

9. ○ cl ○ fl ○ pl

Dictation

1. _____ 2. _____ 3. _____

Skill: Discriminating initial consonant blends **59**

Listen for It

Focus Two consonant sounds said together are called a **consonant blend**. Many words begin with a **consonant + r** blend.

br brave	**dr** drill	**gr** grin	**tr** trade

Say the picture name.
Then fill in the circle next to the blend you hear at the **beginning**.

1.
○ br
○ dr
○ tr

2.
○ br
○ dr
○ tr

3.
○ br
○ gr
○ tr

4.
○ br
○ gr
○ tr

5.
○ br
○ dr
○ tr

6.
○ br
○ dr
○ tr

7.
○ br
○ dr
○ tr

8.
○ br
○ dr
○ tr

9.
○ br
○ dr
○ tr

Dictation •

1. _____   2. _____   3. _____

Write It and Read It

Letter Box

| cl | fl | gl | pl | br | dr | gr | tr |

Say the picture name.
Then write the blend to spell the word.

1. ___ ___ ee	2. 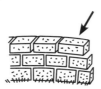 ___ ___ ick	3. ___ ___ apes
4. ___ ___ obe	5. ___ ___ ug	6. ___ ___ ame

Write the words that complete the sentence.
Then read the sentence.

1. clap   flap   flip

Will you _____ when I do a _____?

2. drum   grin   grip

Fran will _____ when she sees her new _____.

Dictation

_____

Listen for It

Focus Some consonant blends begin with the letter **s**. These blends can have one or two consonants after the **s**.

sk	sl	sp	sw	spl	str
skip	**sl**am	**sp**ell	**sw**im	**spl**it	**str**ipe

Say the picture name.
Then fill in the circle next to the blend you hear at the **beginning**.

1.
 ○ sk
 ○ sl
 ○ sp

2.
 ○ sw
 ○ spl
 ○ str

3.
 ○ sk
 ○ sl
 ○ sp

4.
 ○ sk
 ○ sl
 ○ sp

5.
 ○ sw
 ○ spl
 ○ str

6.
 ○ spl
 ○ sl
 ○ sp

7.
 ○ sk
 ○ sl
 ○ sp

8.
 ○ sw
 ○ spl
 ○ str

9.
 ○ sw
 ○ spl
 ○ str

Dictation ··

1. _____ 2. _____ 3. _____ 4. _____

Skill: Writing initial consonant s-blends

Write It and Read It

Letter Box

| sk | sl | sp | sw | spl | str |

Say the picture name.
Then write the blend to spell the word.

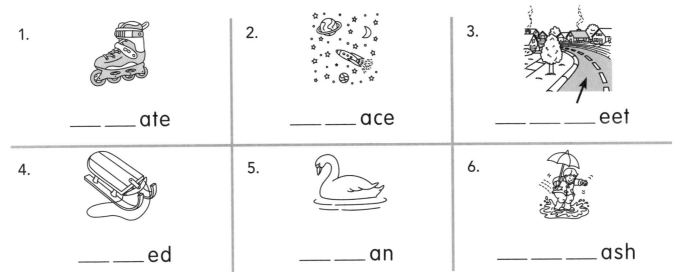

1. ___ ___ate

2. ___ ___ace

3. ___ ___ ___eet

4. ___ ___ed

5. ___ ___an

6. ___ ___ ___ash

Write the words that complete the sentence.
Then read the sentence.

1. slim   splash   swim

Stella can _____ and _____ .

2. stripe   split   skunk

A _____ has a wide _____ on its back.

Dictation ●

_____

Final Consonant Blends
ft, lt, nt, st, ld, nd, mp, nk

DAY 1 **Listening for Final Consonant Blends: ft, lt, nt, st**

Read aloud the focus statement. Then point to the first example as you say: *The letters **f** and **t** blend together to make this sound: /ft/. Say /ft/. (/ft/) You hear /ft/ at the end of **soft**. Say **soft**. (soft)* Repeat this process for the remaining examples. Then read the directions and call students' attention to number 1. Say: *Point to the gift. Say **gift**. (gift) What blend do you hear at the <u>end</u> of **gift**? (/ft/) Which letters stand for /ft/? (ft) Fill in the circle next to the letters **ft**.* Repeat this process for the remaining pictures.
Picture Key: 1. gift, 2. salt, 3. belt, 4. fist, 5. raft, 6. tent, 7. chest, 8. giant, 9. plant

Dictation Direct students' attention to the bottom of the page and say:

Listen to each word I say. Then write the word you hear.   1. *fist*   2. *belt*   3. *raft*   4. *tent*

DAY 2 **Writing Final Consonant Blends: ft, lt, nt, st**

Direct students' attention to the letter box and have them review the sounds that each blend stands for. Then read aloud the directions and call attention to number 1. Say: *Point to the nest. Say **nest**. What blend do you hear at the <u>end</u> of **nest**? (/st/) Which letters stand for /st/? (st) Write **st** to spell the word **nest**. Now let's read the word together: **nest**.* Repeat this process for the remaining pictures.

Dictation Direct students' attention to the bottom of the page and say:

Listen to this sentence: **The vest felt soft.** *Write the words on the line.*

DAY 3 **Listening for Final Consonant Blends: ld, nd, mp, nk**

Read aloud the focus statement. Then point to the first example as you say: *The letters **l** and **d** blend together to make this sound: /ld/. Say /ld/. (/ld/) You hear /ld/ at the end of **hold**. Say **hold**. (hold)* Repeat this process for the remaining examples. Then read the directions and call students' attention to number 1. Say: *Point to the hand. What blend do you hear at the <u>end</u> of **hand**? (/nd/) Which letters stand for /nd/? (nd) Fill in the circle next to the letters **nd**.* Repeat this process for the remaining pictures.
Picture Key: 1. hand, 2. skunk, 3. lamp, 4. cold, 5. stamp, 6. child, 7. chimp, 8. wink, 9. sand

Dictation Direct students' attention to the bottom of the page and say:

Listen to each word I say. Then write the word you hear.   1. *cold*   2. *lamp*   3. *hand*   4. *skunk*

DAY 4 **Writing Final Consonant Blends: ld, nd, mp, nk**

Direct students' attention to the letter box and have them review the sounds that each blend stands for. Then read aloud the directions and call students' attention to number 1. Say: *Point to the hand. Say **hand**. (hand) What blend do you hear at the <u>end</u> of **hand**? (/nd/) Which letters stand for /nd/? (nd) Write **nd** to spell the word **hand**. Now let's read the word together: **hand**.* Repeat this process for the remaining pictures.

Dictation Direct students' attention to the bottom of the page and say:

Listen to this sentence: **I was cold in my tent.** *Write the words on the line.*

DAY 5 **Reading Words with Final Consonant Blends: ft, lt, nt, st, ld, nd, mp, nk**

Read aloud the directions and call students' attention to number 1. Say: *This picture shows a grandfather winking. Sometimes people call their grandfather "Gramps" for short. Now let's read the word choices together: **link, Gramps, wink**. Now let's read the incomplete sentence together: _____ **likes to** _____ **at me.** Which word belongs on the first line? (Gramps) Write **Gramps** on the line. Which word completes the sentence? (wink) Write the word **wink** to complete the sentence.* After students finish writing, say: *Now let's read the sentence together:* **Gramps likes to wink at me.** Repeat this process for the remaining sentences.

Dictation Direct students' attention to the bottom of the page and say:

Listen to this sentence: **He left his belt at home.** *Write the words on the line.*

Listen for It

Focus A consonant blend may be at the end of a word.
Many words end with a **consonant + t** blend.

| **ft** soft | **lt** felt | **nt** mint | **st** mist |

Say the picture name.
Then fill in the circle next to the blend you hear at the **end** of the word.

1.
- ○ ft
- ○ lt
- ○ st

2.
- ○ ft
- ○ lt
- ○ st

3.
- ○ ft
- ○ lt
- ○ nt

4.
- ○ ft
- ○ nt
- ○ st

5.
- ○ ft
- ○ lt
- ○ nt

6.
- ○ ft
- ○ lt
- ○ nt

7.
- ○ ft
- ○ lt
- ○ st

8.
- ○ ft
- ○ nt
- ○ st

9.
- ○ ft
- ○ nt
- ○ st

Dictation •

1. _____   2. _____   3. _____   4. _____

Skill: Discriminating final consonant blends

Write It

Letter Box

ft   lt   nt   st

Say the picture name. Write the blend to spell the word.
Then read the word.

1. ne ___ ___	2. gi ___ ___	3. te ___ ___
4. be ___ ___	5. ra ___ ___	6. me ___ ___
7. cru ___ ___	8. ce ___ ___	9. ca ___ ___

Dictation

_____

Listen for It

Focus — A consonant blend may be at the end of a word. Many words end with the consonant blends **ld**, **nd**, **mp**, or **nk**.

ld	nd	mp	nk
ho**ld**	be**nd**	pu**mp**	pi**nk**

Say the picture name.
Then fill in the circle next to the blend you hear at the **end** of the word.

1. ○ ld ○ mp ○ nd	2.  ○ ld ○ mp ○ nk	3. ○ ld ○ mp ○ nd
4. ○ ld ○ nd ○ mp	5. ○ ld ○ mp ○ nk	6.  ○ ld ○ nd ○ nk
7. ○ ld ○ nd ○ mp	8. ○ ld ○ nk ○ nd	9. ○ ld ○ nk ○ nd

Dictation

1. _____ 2. _____ 3. _____ 4. _____

Skill: Discriminating final consonant blends

Write It

Letter Box

| ld | nd | mp | nk |

Say the picture name. Write the blend to spell the word.
Then read the word.

1.

ha ___ ___

2.

sku ___ ___

3.

la ___ ___

4.

co ___ ___

5.

sta ___ ___

6.

chi ___ ___

7.

chi ___ ___

8.

wi ___ ___

9.

sa ___ ___

Dictation

_____

Read It

Write the words that complete the sentence.
Then read the sentence out loud.

1.

link   Gramps   wink

_____ likes to _____ at me.

2.

gold   hold   host

The chest can _____ a lot of _____.

3.

hand   bunk   bump

How did you get a _____ on your _____?

4.

lift   tent   blimp

The _____ will fly over the _____.

5.

send   spent   band

We _____ time with the _____.

Dictation ●

_____

Consonant Digraphs
ch, sh, th, wh

DAY 1 **Listening for Initial Digraphs**

Read aloud the focus statement. Then point to the first example and say: *The letters c and h together have this sound: /ch/. Say /ch/. (/ch/) You hear /ch/ in the word chip. Say chip.* (chip) Repeat this process for the remaining examples. Then read the directions and call students' attention to number 1. Say: *Point to the chair. Say chair.* (chair) *Do you hear /ch/ in chair?* (yes) *Fill in the circle.* Repeat this process for the remaining pictures.

Picture Key: Row 1: chair, whale, cheese, chest; Row 2: shovel, share, cherry, shell; Row 3: thread, thumb, brush, three; Row 4: whale, sheep, wheel, shirt

Dictation Direct students' attention to the bottom of the page and say:

Listen to each word I say. Then write the letters that stand for the <u>first</u> sound you hear.
1. shine   2. thing   3. chose   4. while

DAY 2 **Writing Initial Digraphs**

Read aloud the directions and call students' attention to number 1. Say: *Point to the shirt. Say shirt.* (shirt) *What sound do you hear at the beginning of shirt?* (/sh/) *Which letters stand for that sound?* (sh) *Write the letters sh on the lines to spell the word shirt.* Repeat this process for the remaining pictures.

Picture Key: 1. shirt, 2. whale, 3. cherry, 4. chain, 5. shell, 6. three, 7. shave, 8. chest, 9. wheel, 10. wheat, 11. thunder, 12. shrimp

Dictation Direct students' attention to the bottom of the page and say:

Listen to each word I say. Then write the word on the line.   *1. shake   2. chunk   3. thump   4. white*

DAY 3 **Listening for Final Digraphs**

Read aloud the focus statement. Then point to the first example and say: *What sound do the letters ch have?* (/ch/) *You hear /ch/ at the <u>end</u> of the word rich. Say rich.* (rich) Repeat this process for the remaining examples. Then read the directions and call students' attention to number 1. Say: *Point to the bench. Say bench.* (bench) *Do you hear /ch/ in bench?* (yes) *Fill in the circle.* Repeat this process for the remaining rows.

Picture Key: Row 1: bench, sock, peach, sandwich; Row 2: wash, trash, lock, fish; Row 3: tooth, math, bath, foot

Dictation Direct students' attention to the bottom of the page and say:

Listen to each word I say. Then write the letters that stand for the <u>last</u> sound you hear.
1. cash   2. such   3. cloth

DAY 4 **Writing Ending Digraphs**

Read aloud the directions and call students' attention to number 1. Say: *Point to the picture of a person washing dishes. Say wash.* (wash) *What sound do you hear at the <u>end</u> of wash?* (/sh/) *Which letters stand for that sound?* (sh) *Write the letters sh on the lines to spell the word wash.* Repeat this process for the remaining pictures.

Picture Key: 1. wash, 2. peach, 3. bath, 4. bench, 5. tooth, 6. trash, 7. sandwich, 8. moth, 9. fish, 10. path, 11. bush, 12. inch

Dictation Direct students' attention to the bottom of the page and say:

Listen to each word I say. Then write the word on the line.   *1. math   2. fresh   3. bunch*

DAY 5 **Reading Words with Digraphs**

Read aloud the directions and call students' attention to number 1. Say: *Two words are missing from this sentence. Let's read the sentence together: We _____ have to _____ the dog. Now let's read the word choices together: both, wash. Which word belongs on the first line?* (both) *Write the word both on the line. Which word belongs on the second line?* (wash) *Write wash.* After students finish writing, say: *Now let's read the sentence together: We both have to wash the dog.* Repeat this process for the remaining sentences.

Dictation Direct students' attention to the bottom of the page and say:

Listen to this sentence: She will brush her teeth. Write the words on the line.

Listen for It

Focus A digraph is two letters together that have one new sound. Many words begin with a **consonant + h** digraph.

| ch **ch**ip | sh **sh**ut | th **th**in | wh **wh**en |

Say the sound of the two letters. Then say each picture name.
Fill in the circle if the picture name **begins** with that sound.

1. ch-

○   ○   ○   ○

2. sh-

○   ○   ○   ○

3. th-

○   ○   ○   ○

4. wh-

○   ○   ○   ○

Dictation ···

1. ___ ___ine   2. ___ ___ing   3. ___ ___ose   4. ___ ___ile

Write It

Letter Box

ch   sh   th   wh

Say the picture name. Listen to the **first** sound.
Then write the missing letters to spell the word.

1. ____ ____irt

2. ____ ____ale

3. ____ ____erry

4. ____ ____ain

5. ____ ____ell

6. ____ ____ree

7. ____ ____ave

8. ____ ____est

9. ____ ____eel

10. ____ ____eat

11. ____ ____under

12. ____ ____rimp

Dictation ....

1. _____   2. _____   3. _____   4. _____

Listen for It

Focus A digraph may begin or end a word. Many words end with the digraph **ch**, **sh**, or **th**.

| ch ri**ch** | sh ra**sh** | th bo**th** |

Say the sound of the two letters. Then say each picture name.
Fill in the circle if the picture name **ends** with that sound.

1. -ch ○   ○   ○   ○

2. -sh ○   ○   ○   ○

3. -th ○ $$\begin{array}{r} 2 \\ +4 \\ \hline 6 \end{array}$$ ○   ○   ○

Dictation •

1. ca_____   2. su_____   3. clo_____

Skill: Discriminating final consonant digraphs

Write It

Letter Box

ch   sh   th

Say the picture name. Listen to the **last sound**.
Then write the missing letters to spell the word.

1. wa____ ____

2. pea____ ____

3. ba____ ____

4. ben____ ____

5. too____ ____

6. tra____ ____

7. sandwi____ ____

8. mo____ ____

9. fi____ ____

10. pa____ ____

11. bu____ ____

12. in____ ____

Dictation

1. _____   2. _____   3. _____

Read It

Write the words that complete the sentence.
Then read the sentence out loud.

1.   both   wash

   We _____ have to _____ the dog.

2.   bush   moth

   A white _____ landed on the _____.

3.   ranch   sheep

   A flock of _____ live on that _____.

4.   chimp   think

   I _____ I see a _____.

5.   teeth   whale

   Does a _____ have _____?

Dictation •

_____

Consonant Digraphs
ph, gh, ck, ng

DAY 1

Listening for Consonant Digraphs: ph, gh

Read aloud the focus statement. Then point to the first example and have students say **phone**. Explain: *The /f/ sound you hear in* **phone** *is spelled with the letters* **ph**. Repeat this process for **gh**. Point out that the letters **gh** usually come at the <u>end</u> of a word. Then read the directions and call students' attention to number 1. Say: *Point to the trophy. Now run your finger under the letters as we read the word together:* **trophy**. *Which two letters have the /f/ sound?* (ph) *Underline the letters* **ph**. Repeat this process for the remaining words.

Dictation   Direct students' attention to the bottom of the page and say:

Listen to each word I say. Then write the missing letters to complete the word.
1. cough   2. photo   3. elephant   4. laugh

DAY 2

Writing Words with Consonant Digraphs: ph, gh

Read aloud the directions and call students' attention to the word box. Have students read each word aloud with you. Then point to number 1 and say: *Say* **phone**. (phone) *What sound do you hear at the beginning of* **phone**? (/f/) *Look at the word box and find the word* **phone**. *Which digraph stands for the /f/ sound in* **phone**? (ph) *Write the letters* **ph** *on the lines to spell the word* **phone**. Repeat this process for the remaining pictures.

Picture Key: 1. phone, 2. trophy, 3. cough, 4. dolphin, 5. photo, 6. elephant, 7. graph, 8. laugh, 9. alphabet

Dictation   Direct students' attention to the bottom of the page and say:

Listen to each word I say. Then write the missing letters to complete the word.
1. enough   2. rough   3. trophy   4. photo

DAY 3

Listening for Consonant Digraphs: ck, ng

Read aloud the focus statement. Then point to the first example and have students say **clock**. Say: *The /k/ sound you hear at the end of* **clock** *is spelled* **ck**. Point out that the letters **ck** usually come at the end of a word. Repeat this process for the digraph **ng**. Then read the directions and call students' attention to number 1. Say: *Say* **sock**. (sock) *What sound do you hear at the <u>end</u> of* **sock**? (/k/) *What two letters stand for /k/ in* **sock**? (ck) *Fill in the circle next to the letters* **ck**. Repeat this process for the remaining pictures.

Picture Key: 1. sock, 2. truck, 3. king, 4. brick, 5. wing, 6. peacock, 7. swing, 8. lung, 9. check

Dictation   Direct students' attention to the bottom of the page and say:

Listen to each word I say. Then write the letters that stand for the sounds you hear.
1. sock   2. wing   3. lung   4. brick

DAY 4

Writing Words with Consonant Digraphs: ck, ng

Read the directions and call students' attention to the word box. Have students read each word aloud with you. Then call students' attention to number 1. Say: *Point to the king. Say* **king**. (king) *What sound do you hear at the <u>end</u> of* **king**? (/ng/) *Find the word* **king** *in the word box and write it on the line. Now let's read the word together:* **king**. Repeat this process for the remaining words.

Picture Key: 1. king, 2. lock, 3. brick, 4. lung, 5. truck, 6. ring, 7. neck, 8. sing, 9. clock

Dictation   Direct students' attention to the bottom of the page and say:

Listen to each word I say. Then write the word you hear.   *1. sick   2. trick   3. thing   4. sting*

DAY 5

Reading Words with Consonant Digraphs: ph, gh, ck, ng

Read the directions and call students' attention to number 1. Say: *Let's read the word choices:* **sang, song, sing**. *Now let's read the incomplete sentence:* **Which _____ did she _____?** *Which word belongs on the first line?* (song) *Write* **song** *on the line. Which word belongs on the second line?* (sing) *Write* **sing** *to complete the sentence.* After students finish writing, say: *Now let's read the sentence together:* **Which song did she sing?** Repeat this process for the remaining sentences.

Dictation   Direct students' attention to the bottom of the page and say:

Listen to this sentence: **Pick the phone you like best.** *Write the words on the line.*

Listen for It

Focus A digraph is two letters together that have one sound. The digraphs **ph** and **gh** usually have the **/f/** sound.

ph		**ph**one	**gh**		lau**gh**

Say the picture name. Read the word.
Then underline the two letters that have the **/f/** sound.

1.

trophy

2.

photo

3.

cough

4.
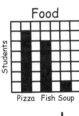
graph

5.

rough

6.

gopher

7.

alphabet

8.

sphere

9.

elephant

Dictation ··

1. cou____ ____   2. ____ ____oto   3. ele____ ____ant   4. lau____ ____

Write It

Word Box

trophy	phone	elephant
alphabet	cough	graph
photo	dolphin	laugh

Write the missing letters to complete the word.
Then read the word.

1.

___ ___ one

2.

tro ___ ___ y

3.

cou ___ ___

4.

dol ___ ___ in

5.

___ ___ oto

6.

ele ___ ___ ant

7.

gra ___ ___

8.

lau ___ ___

9.

al ___ ___ abet

Dictation

1. enou ___ ___   2. rou ___ ___   3. tro ___ ___ y   4. ___ ___ oto

Listen for It

Focus The letter pairs **ck** and **ng** are digraphs. The **ck** digraph has the /k/ sound. The **ng** digraph has the sound you hear at the end of **ring**. Many words end with these digraphs.

ck		clo**ck**	ng		ri**ng**

Say the picture name.
Then fill in the circle next to the digraph you hear at the **end** of the word.

1.
   ○ **ck**
   ○ **ng**

2.
   ○ **ck**
   ○ **ng**

3.
   ○ **ck**
   ○ **ng**

4.
   ○ **ck**
   ○ **ng**

5.
   ○ **ck**
   ○ **ng**

6.
   ○ **ck**
   ○ **ng**

7.
   ○ **ck**
   ○ **ng**

8.
   ○ **ck**
   ○ **ng**

9.
   ○ **ck**
   ○ **ng**

Dictation •

1. _____ 2. _____ 3. _____ 4. _____

Write It

Word Box

king	brick	lung
neck	clock	lock
ring	sing	truck

Say the picture name. Then write the word that names the picture.

1.

_____

2.

_____

3.

_____

4.

_____

5.

_____

6.

_____

7.

_____

8.

_____

9.

_____

Dictation

1. _____   2. _____   3. _____   4. _____

Read It

Write the words that complete the sentence.
Then read the sentence.

1.   sang   song   sing

Which _____ did she _____?

2.   bang   sock   hang

I will _____ my wet _____ to dry.

3.   sting   neck   brick

Mick has a bee _____ on his _____.

4.   belong   along   dolphin

Does a _____ _____ in a tank?

5.   laugh   photo   tough

This _____ of me will make you _____!

Dictation ···

_____

DAY 1 — **Listening for the Sound of /j/**

Read aloud the focus statement. Point to the example word and say: *This word says **badge**. Say **badge**.* (badge) *What sound do the letters **dge** have at the end of **badge**?* (/j/) Then read the directions and call students' attention to number 1. Say: *Point to the bridge. Say **bridge**.* (bridge) *Is /**j**/ the last sound in **bridge**?* (yes) *Fill in the circle next to **yes**. Now point to the boot. Say **boot**.* (boot) *Is /**j**/ the last sound in **boot**?* (no) *Fill in the circle next to **no**.* Repeat this process for the remaining pictures.

Picture Key: 1. bridge, 2. boot, 3. wedge, 4. jeans, 5. lamp, 6. hedge, 7. nudge, 8. corn, 9. judge

Dictation Direct students' attention to the bottom of the page and say:
Listen to each word I say. Then write the missing letters. 1. nudge 2. hedge 3. wedge 4. bridge

DAY 2 — **Writing Words Ending in dge**

Call students' attention to the word box at the top of the page. Have students read each word aloud with you. Then read the directions and call students' attention to number 1. Say: *This picture shows a plate of fudge. Say **fudge**.* (fudge) *Find the word **fudge** in the word box. How is **fudge** spelled?* (f-u-d-g-e) *Write the word **fudge** on the line.* Repeat this process for the remaining pictures.

Picture Key: 1. fudge, 2. bridge, 3. hedge, 4. judge, 5. fridge, 6. badge, 7. wedge, 8. nudge, 9. pledge

Dictation Direct students' attention to the bottom of the page and say:
Listen to each word I say. Then write the missing letters. 1. edge 2. lodge 3. ridge 4. dodge

DAY 3 — **Listening for the /ch/ Sound**

Read aloud the focus statement. Point to the example word and say: *This word says **watch**. Say **watch**.* (watch) *The letters **tch** have the /**ch**/ sound at the end of **watch**. Say /**ch**/.* (/ch/) Then read the directions and call students' attention to number 1. Say: *Point to the picture of a boy scratching an itch. Say **itch**.* (itch) *Is /**ch**/ the last sound in **itch**?* (yes) *Fill in the circle next to **yes**. Now point to the pretzel. Say **pretzel**.* (pretzel) *Is /**ch**/ the last sound in **pretzel**?* (no) *Fill in the circle next to **no**.* Repeat this process for the remaining pictures.

Picture Key: 1. itch, 2. pretzel, 3. pitch, 4. patch, 5. catch, 6. brush, 7. fist, 8. match, 9. stretch

Dictation Direct students' attention to the bottom of the page and say:
Listen to each word I say. Then write the missing letters. 1. pitch 2. match 3. stretch

DAY 4 — **Writing Words Spelled with tch**

Call students' attention to the word box at the top of the page. Have students read each word aloud with you. Then read the directions and call students' attention to number 1. Say: *This picture shows someone catching a ball. Say **catch**.* (catch) *Find the word **catch** in the word box. How is **catch** spelled?* (c-a-t-c-h) *Write the word **catch** on the line.* Repeat this process for the remaining pictures.

Picture Key: 1. catch, 2. itch, 3. crutch, 4. ditch, 5. pitch, 6. hatch, 7. witch, 8. kitchen, 9. switch

Dictation Direct students' attention to the bottom of the page and say:
Listen to this sentence: ***Watch out for that ditch!*** *Write the words on the line.*

DAY 5 — **Reading Words with Variant Spellings of /j/ and /ch/: dge, tch**

Read aloud the directions and then call students' attention to number 1. Say: *Let's read the incomplete sentence together:* ***Is the _____ in the fridge?*** *Now let's read the two word choices:* **nudge, fudge**. *Which word completes the sentence?* (fudge) *Write **fudge** on the line.* After students finish writing, say: *Now let's read the sentence together:* ***Is the fudge in the fridge?*** Repeat this process for the remaining sentences.

Dictation Direct students' attention to the bottom of the page and say:
Listen to this sentence: ***The latch will not budge!*** *Write the words on the line.*

Listen for It

Focus The letters **dge** at the end of a word have the /j/ sound.

ba**dge**

Say the picture name.
Fill in the circle next to **yes** if the final sound is **/j/**.
Fill in the circle next to **no** if the final sound is <u>not</u> **/j/**.

1.

○ yes   ○ no

2.

○ yes   ○ no

3.

○ yes   ○ no

4.

○ yes   ○ no

5.

○ yes   ○ no

6.

○ yes   ○ no

7.

○ yes   ○ no

8.

○ yes   ○ no

9.

○ yes   ○ no

Dictation ....

1. ___ ___ dge   2. ___ ___ dge   3. ___ ___ dge   4. ___ ___ dge

Write It

Word Box

badge	fudge	nudge
bridge	hedge	pledge
fridge	judge	wedge

Say the picture name. Then write the word on the line.

1.

   _____

2.

   _____

3.

   _____

4.

   _____

5.

   _____

6.

   _____

7.

   _____

8.

   _____

9.

   _____

Dictation ....

1. ___dge   2. _____dge   3. _____dge   4. _____dge

Listen for It

Focus The sound **/ch/** can be spelled with the letters **tch**.

wa**tch**

Say the picture name.
Fill in the circle next to **yes** if the final sound is **/ch/**.
Fill in the circle next to **no** if the final sound is <u>not</u> **/ch/**.

1.  ○ yes ○ no	2. ○ yes ○ no	3.  ○ yes ○ no
4. ○ yes ○ no	5.  ○ yes ○ no	6. ○ yes ○ no
7.  ○ yes ○ no	8. ○ yes ○ no	9.  ○ yes ○ no

Dictation ••

1. ___ ___tch   2. ___ ___tch   3. ___ ___ ___tch

Skill: Discriminating the **/ch/** sound   **85**

Write It

Word Box

catch	hatch	pitch
crutch	itch	switch
ditch	kitchen	witch

Say the picture name. Then write the word on the line.

1.

_____

2.

_____

3.

_____

4.

_____

5.

_____

6.

_____

7.

_____

8.

_____

9.

_____

Dictation

....

_____

Read It

Write the word that completes the sentence.
Then read the sentence out loud.

1. Is the _____ in the fridge?

   nudge   fudge

2. You _____ the ball, and I will catch it.

   patch   pitch

3. A _____ gave me a trophy at the end of the match.

   judge   budge

4. My dog will _____ the stick by the hedge.

   sketch   fetch

5. Do not stand at the _____ of the ledge.

   badge   edge

6. Does your badge _____ my badge?

   match   hatch

Dictation ··

_____

Silent Consonants
k, w, b, h, l

DAY 1

Discerning Silent Letters: k, w

Read aloud the focus statement. Then point to the first example and say: *This word says* **knee**. *Say* **knee**. (knee) *Do you hear /k/ at the beginning of* **knee**? (no) *What sound do you hear?* (/n/) *That's right. The letter* **k** *is silent. Repeat this process for* **write**. *Then read the directions and call students' attention to number 1. Say: Point to the knot. Say* **knot**. (knot) *Which letter in* **knot** *is silent?* (k) *Draw a line through the* **k**. *Repeat this process for the remaining words.*

Dictation Direct students' attention to the bottom of the page and say:

Listen to each word I say. Then write the missing letters to complete the word you hear.
1. knob   2. wrote   3. wrong

DAY 2

Discerning Silent Letters: b, h

Read aloud the focus statement. Then point to the first example and say: *This word says* **comb**. *Say* **comb**. (comb) *Do you hear /b/ in* **comb**? (no) *That's right. The letter* **b** *is silent. Repeat the process for* **rhyme**. *Then read the directions and call students' attention to number 1. Say: Point to the lamb. Say* **lamb**. (lamb) *Which letter in* **lamb** *is silent?* (b) *Draw a line through the* **b**. *Repeat this process for the remaining words.*

Dictation Direct students' attention to the bottom of the page and say:

Listen to each word I say. Then write the word you hear.   *1. limb   2. hour (as in telling time)   3. thumb*

DAY 3

Discerning Silent Letter: l

Read aloud the focus statement. Then point to the first example and say: *This word says* **calf**. *Say* **calf**. (calf) *Do you hear /l/ in* **calf**? (no) *That's right. The letter* **l** *is silent. Then read the directions and call students' attention to number 1. Say: Point to the people walking. Say* **walk**. (walk) *Which letter in* **walk** *is silent?* (l) *Draw a line through the* **l**. *Repeat this process for the remaining words.*

Dictation Direct students' attention to the bottom of the page and say:

Listen to each word I say. Then write the word you hear.   *1. half   2. chalk   3. calves*

DAY 4

Writing Words with Silent Letters: k, w, b, h, l

Call students' attention to the word box at the top of the page. Have students read each word aloud with you. Then read the directions and call students' attention to number 1. Say: *This picture shows people walking. Say* **walk**. (walk) *Find the word* **walk** *in the word box. How is* **walk** *spelled?* (w-a-l-k) *Write the word* **walk** *on the line. Repeat this process for the remaining pictures.*

Picture Key: 1. walk, 2. yolk, 3. wrap, 4. comb, 5. thumb, 6. knee, 7. knit, 8. rhino, 9. talk

Dictation Direct students' attention to the bottom of the page and say:

Listen to each word I say. Then write the word you hear.   *1. ghost   2. knit   3. wreck*

DAY 5

Reading Words with Silent Letters: k, w, b, h, l

Read the directions and call students' attention to number 1. Say: *Let's read the word choices:* **half, calf, knife**. *Now let's read the incomplete sentence together: Use a _____ to cut the cake in _____. Which word belongs on the first line?* (knife) *Write* **knife** *on the line. Which word belongs on the second line?* (half) *Write the word* **half** *to complete the sentence. After students finish writing, say: Now let's read the sentence together:* **Use a knife to cut the cake in half.** *Repeat this process for the remaining sentences.*

Dictation Direct students' attention to the bottom of the page and say:

Listen to this sentence: **Does a ghost need a comb?** *Write the words on the line.*

Listen for It

Focus Sometimes a consonant is **silent**, or does not have a sound.
In words beginning with **kn**, the k is usually silent.
In words beginning with **wr**, the w is usually silent.

knee   **w**rite

Say the picture name. Listen to the letter-sounds.
Then cross out the **silent** consonant in the word.

1. knot	2. wrap	3. kneel
4. wrist	5. knife	6. knock
7. knit	8.  wreck	9. wrench

Dictation ••

1. k_____   2. w_____   3. w_____

Listen for It

Focus   Sometimes the consonants **b** and **h** are **silent**.

 |

com**b**   r**h**yme

Say the picture name. Listen to the letter-sounds.
Then cross out the **silent** consonant in the word.

1. lamb	2. ghost	3. thumb
4. hour	5. limb	6. crumb
7.  climb	8.  rhino	9.  plumber

Dictation •

1. _____   2. _____   3. _____

Listen for It

Focus When the letter **l** comes before **f**, **v**, or **k**, the **l** can be silent.

calf
ca~~l~~f

Say the picture name. Listen to the letter-sounds.
Then cross out the **silent** consonant in the word.

1.

walk

2.

half

3.

yolk

4.

calves

5.

chalk

6.

polka dot

7.

talk

8.

stalk

9.

halves

Dictation ....

1. _____   2. _____   3. _____

Skill: Discriminating silent letters in words   **91**

Name _____

Write It

Word Box

thumb	rhino	yolk
wrap	knit	comb
walk	knee	talk

Say the picture name. Then write the word on the line.

1.

_____

2.

_____

3.

_____

4.

_____

5.

_____

6.

_____

7.

_____

8.

_____

9.

_____

Dictation

1. _____   2. _____   3. _____

Read It

Write the words that complete the sentence.
Then read the sentence out loud.

1.   half   calf   knife

Use a _____ to cut the cake in _____.

2.   climb   walk   crumb

You can _____ up the path and _____ the hill.

3.   crumb   lamb   thumb

Pick up the _____ with your _____.

4.   wrote   chalk   wrap

Anna _____ her name with white _____.

5.   knot   rhino   knock

A _____ can _____ down a tree!

Dictation •

_____

Long Vowel Digraphs
ai, ay

DAY 1 **Listening for Long a Digraphs**

Read aloud the focus statement. Then point to the first example and say: *The vowels **a** and **i** together have the **long a** sound: /ā/. You hear /ā/ in **tail**. Say **tail**.* (tail) Repeat this process for the letters **a** and **y** in **tray**. Then read the directions and call students' attention to number 1. Say: *Point to the nail. Say **nail**.* (nail) *Do you hear /ā/ in **nail**?* (yes) *Which letters have the **long a** sound?* (ai) *Underline the letters **ai** in **nail**.* Repeat this process for the remaining words.

Dictation   Direct students' attention to the bottom of the page and say:

Listen to each word I say. Then write the word you hear.   1. clay   2. brain   3. snail

DAY 2 **Listening for Long a Digraphs**

Direct students' attention to the letter box at the top of the page. Remind students that **ai** usually comes in the middle of a word and **ay** at the end of a word. Then read the directions and call students' attention to number 1. Say: *The picture shows a monkey. The arrow is pointing to its tail. Say **tail**.* (tail) *Do you hear the **long a** sound in **tail**?* (yes) *Where?* (in the middle) *Which two letters usually spell the **long a** sound in the middle of a word?* (ai) *Write the letters **ai** on the line. Now let's read the word together: **tail**.* Repeat this process for the remaining words.

Dictation   Direct students' attention to the bottom of the page and say:

Listen to each word I say. Then write the word you hear.   1. nail   2. sway   3. pain

DAY 3 **Writing Words with Long a Digraphs**

Call students' attention to the word box at the top of the page. Have students read each word aloud. Then read the directions and call students' attention to number 1. Say: *The picture shows a tray. Find the word **tray** in the word box. How is **tray** spelled?* (t-r-a-y) *Write the word **tray** on the line under the picture. Circle the letters that have the **long a** sound.* Repeat this process for the remaining pictures.

Picture Key: 1. tray, 2. pail, 3. paint, 4. jay, 5. pay, 6. trail, 7. chain, 8. freeway, 9. braid

Dictation   Direct students' attention to the bottom of the page and say:

Listen to each word I say. Then write the word you hear.   1. rail   2. runway   3. stain

DAY 4 **Reading Words with Long a Digraphs**

Read the directions and call students' attention to phrase number 1. Say: *Let's read number 1 together: **stack of hay**. Which letters have the **long a** sound in **hay**?* (ay) *Underline those letters. Which picture goes with these words?* (the haystack) *Draw a line from the word **hay** to the picture of the haystack.* Repeat this process for the remaining phrases.

Dictation   Direct students' attention to the bottom of the page and say:

*Listen to this sentence: **Take the subway to Main Street.** Write the words on the line.*

DAY 5 **Reading Words with Long a Digraphs**

Read the directions and call students' attention to number 1. Say: *Let's read the incomplete sentence together: **This toy train is made from _____**. Now let's read the two word choices: **play, clay**. Which word completes the sentence?* (clay) *Yes. A toy train can be made of clay. Write **clay** on the line.* After students finish writing, say: *Now let's read the sentence together: **This toy train is made from clay.*** Repeat this process for the remaining sentences.

Dictation   Direct students' attention to the bottom of the page and say:

*Listen to this sentence: **We must pay to ride the train.** Write the words on the line.*

Listen for It

Focus

The vowel pairs **ai** and **ay** are digraphs that have the **long a** sound. The vowels **ai** usually come in the **middle** of a word. The vowels **ay** usually come at the **end** of a word.

long **a**
t**ai**l	tr**ay**

Say the picture name. Read the word.
Then underline the two letters that stand for the **long a** sound.

1. nail	2. hay	3. rain
4. mail	5. clay	6. brain
7. snail	8. paid	9. X-ray

Dictation •••

1. _____   2. _____   3. _____

Skill: Identifying **long a** digraphs

Listen for It

Letter Box

ai   ay

Say the picture name.
Then write the letters that spell the word.

1.

t ____ l

2.

cl ____

3.

r ____ n

4.

tr ____ n

5.

n ____ l

6.

sn ____ l

7.

j ____

8.

p ____ nt

9.

subw ____

10.

m ____ l

11.

ch ____ n

12.

br ____ d

Dictation ·

1. _____   2. _____   3. _____

Write It

Word Box

paint	tray	pay
jay	braid	pail
freeway	chain	trail

Say the picture name. Write the word on the line.
Then circle the letters that have the **long a** sound.

1.
_____

2.
_____

3.
_____

4.
_____

5.
_____

6.
_____

7.
_____

8.
_____

9.
_____

Dictation

1. _____   2. _____   3. _____

Read It

Read the phrase. Underline the letters that have the **long a** sound.
Then draw a line from the words to the correct picture.

1. stack of **hay**

2. **rainy day**

3. **train** on a track

4. **spray paint**

5. tree by the **trail**

6. thick **braid**

7. **freeway** to the city

Dictation

_____

_____

Read It

Write the word that completes each sentence.
Then read the sentence out loud.

1. This toy train is made from _____.

   play   clay

2. Jay likes to chase me in the _____.

   hallway   freeway

3. The snail left a _____ of slime.

   train   trail

4. May I hang my hat on that _____?

   hail   nail

5. How did the dog get _____ on its tail?

   pain   paint

6. I am not afraid to _____ on the lake.

   sail   stain

Dictation ●

_____

Skill: Reading words with **long a** digraphs

Long Vowel Digraphs
ee, ea, ey, ie

DAY 1

Listening for Long e

Read aloud the focus statement. Then point to the first example word and say: *The two e's together have the long e sound: /ē/. You hear /ē/ in **queen**. Say **queen**.* (queen) Repeat this process for the vowels **e** and **a** in **jeans**. Then read the directions and call students' attention to number 1. Say: *Point to the seal. Say **seal**. Do you hear /ē/ in **seal**?* (yes) *Which two letters stand for the **long e** sound?* (ea) *Underline the letters **e** and **a** in **seal**.* Repeat this process for the remaining words.

Dictation   Direct students' attention to the bottom of the page and say:

Listen to each word I say. Then write the missing letters to complete the word.
1. east   2. heel (as in part of your foot)   3. teach

DAY 2

Listening for Long e

Read aloud the focus statement. Then point to the first example word and say: *The letters **e** and **y** together have the **long e** sound: /ē/. You hear /ē/ in **joey**. A joey is a baby kangaroo. Say **joey**.* (joey) Repeat this process for the vowels **i** and **e** in **chief**. Then read the directions and call students' attention to number 1. Say: *Point to the key. Say **key**.* (key) *Do you hear /ē/ in **key**?* (yes) *Which two letters stand for the **long e** sound?* (ey) *Underline the letters **e** and **y** in **key**.* Repeat this process for the remaining words.

Dictation   Direct students' attention to the bottom of the page and say:

Listen to each word I say. Then write the missing letters to complete the word.   *1. brief   2. key   3. grief*

DAY 3

Reading Words with Long e Digraphs

Read the directions and call students' attention to number 1. Say: *Let's read number 1 together: **white bean**. Which letters have the **long e** sound in **bean**?* (ea) *Underline those letters. Which picture goes with these words?* (bean) *Draw a line from the word **bean** to the picture of the bean.* Repeat this process for the remaining phrases.

Dictation   Direct students' attention to the bottom of the page and say:

Listen to each word I say. Then write the missing letters to complete the word.
1. chief   2. speed   3. feast   4. honey

DAY 4

Writing Words with Long e Digraphs

Call students' attention to the word box at the top of the page. Have students read each word aloud. Then read the directions and call students' attention to number 1. Say: *The picture shows a donkey. Look at the word box and find the word **donkey**. Write the word on the line under the picture.* After students have finished writing, say: *Which letters have the **long e** sound in **donkey**?* (ey) *Circle those letters.* Repeat this process for the remaining pictures.

Picture Key: 1. donkey, 2. piece, 3. sweep, 4. seal, 5. beach, 6. honey, 7. jeep, 8. peek, 9. chief

Dictation   Direct students' attention to the bottom of the page and say:

Listen to each word I say. Then write the missing letters to complete the word.
1. reach   2. money   3. greet   3. shield

DAY 5

Reading Words with Long e Digraphs

Call students' attention to the word box at the top of the page. Have students read each word aloud. Then read the directions and call students' attention to number 1. Say: *Let's read the incomplete sentence together: **A thief may steal all of your _____**. Which word best completes the sentence?* (money) *Write the word **money** on the line.* After students finish writing, say: *Now let's read the sentence together: **A thief may steal all of your money**.* Repeat this process for the remaining sentences.

Dictation   Direct students' attention to the bottom of the page and say:

*Listen to this sentence: **The chief has the key to the jeep**. Write the words on the line.*

Listen for It

Focus The vowel pairs **ee** and **ea** are digraphs that often have the **long e** sound.

| long **e** | |
| qu**ee**n | j**ea**ns |

Say the picture name. Read the word.
Then underline the two letters that stand for the **long e** sound.

1. seal	2. feet	3. jeep
4. bean	5. leaf	6. kneel
7. peach	8. sneeze	9. team

Dictation •••

1. ea_____   2. ___ee___   3. ___ea_____

Listen for It

Focus The vowel pairs **ey** and **ie** are digraphs that often have the **long e** sound. The digraph **ey** usually comes at the **end** of a word. The digraph **ie** usually comes in the **middle** of a word.

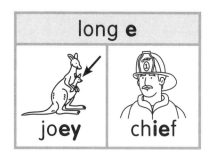

Say the picture name. Read the word.
Then underline the two letters that stand for the **long e** sound.

1. key	2. donkey	3. thief
4. money	5. field	6. monkey
7. honey	8. piece	9. shield

Dictation ·

1. ___ ___ ie ___   2. ___ ey   3. ___ ___ ie ___

Read It

Read each pair of words. Underline the letters that have the **long e** sound.
Then draw a line to the correct picture.

1. white **bean**

2. **sweet honey**

3. big **sneeze**

4. **green field**

5. **deep sleep**

6. sandy **beach**

7. my **team**

8. little **joey**

Dictation

1. ___ ___ie___   2. ___ ___ee___   3. ___ea___ ___   4. ___ ___ ___ey

Skill: Identifying **long e** digraphs

Write It

Word Box

beach	jeep	chief
donkey	honey	peek
piece	seal	sweep

Write the word that names the picture.
Then circle the two letters that stand for the **long e** sound.

1.
_____

2.
_____

3.
_____

4.
_____

5.
_____

6.
_____

7.
_____

8.
_____

9.
_____

Dictation

1. ___ea_____   2. _____ey   3. ___ee___   4. ___ie____

Read It

Word Box

chief	dream	freeze	jeep
money	monkey	peach	piece

Write the word that completes the sentence.
Then read the sentence out loud.

1. A thief may steal all of your _____.

2. A _____ is sweet to eat.

3. A _____ leads a team.

4. Ice cream will melt if you do not _____ it.

5. A _____ can hang from its tail.

6. You _____ when you sleep.

7. I drive my _____ on the field.

8. You can eat a _____ of cheese.

Dictation

_____

Long Vowel Patterns
ie, igh

DAY 1 — Listening for Long i

Read aloud the focus statement. Then point to the word **tie** and say: *We've just learned that the letters i and e together in a word can stand for the long e sound. But they can also stand for the long i sound you hear in the word tie. Say tie.* (tie) Then point to the word **high** and say: *The letters i, g, and h together can also have the long i sound. Say high.* (high) *Do you hear the g in high?* (no) Then read the directions and call students' attention to number 1. Say: *Say pie.* (pie) *Do you hear /ī/ in pie?* (yes) *What letters have the /ī/ sound in pie?* (ie) *Underline the letters i and e in pie.* Repeat this process for the remaining words.

Dictation   Direct students' attention to the bottom of the page and say:

Listen to each word I say. Then write the missing letters to complete the word.
1. right (as in correct)   2. tries   3. bright

DAY 2 — Writing Words Spelled with ie and igh

Read the directions and call students' attention to the word box. Have students read each word aloud. Then say: *Now point to the first word in the box again. What does it say?* (night) *Which letters have the /ī/ sound in night?* (igh) *Write the word night on the line in the box that says igh at the top.* Repeat the process for the remaining words.

Dictation   Direct students' attention to the bottom of the page and say:

Listen to each word I say. Then write the missing letters to complete the word.   *1. dried   2. might   3. fright*

DAY 3 — Writing Words Spelled with ie and igh

Call students' attention to the word box. Have students read each word aloud. Then read the directions and call students' attention to number 1. Say: *The picture shows a fried egg. Say fried.* (fried) *Find the word fried in the word box. How is fried spelled?* (f-r-i-e-d) *Write the word fried on the line under the picture. Circle the letters that have the long i sound.* Repeat this process for the remaining pictures.

Picture Key: 1. fried, 2. high, 3. fight, 4. light, 5. cries, 6. thigh, 7. pie, 8. night, 9. lie

Dictation   Direct students' attention to the bottom of the page and say:

Listen to each word I say. Then write the missing letters to complete the word.   *1. tried   2. sight   3. tight*

DAY 4 — Reading Words Spelled with ie and igh

Read the directions and call students' attention to number 1. Say: *Point to the flies. Say flies.* (flies) *What sounds do you hear first in the word flies?* (/f/ /l/) *What letters stand for the sound of /f/ /l/?* (f and l) *Fill in the circle next to the word that spells flies. Now spell flies out loud.* (f-l-i-e-s) Repeat this process for the remaining words.

Dictation   Direct students' attention to the bottom of the page and say:

Listen to each word I say. Then write the letters that stand for the sounds you hear.   *1. cried   2. flies   3. flight*

DAY 5 — Reading Words Spelled with ie and igh

Read the directions and call students' attention to number 1. Say: *Let's read the incomplete sentence:* **My desk _____ is too _____.** *Now let's read the word choices:* **bright, light, sight.** *Which word belongs on the first line?* (light) *Write light on the line. Which word belongs on the second line?* (bright) *Write the word bright to complete the sentence.* After students finish writing, say: *Now let's read the sentence together:* **My desk light is too bright.** Repeat this process for the remaining sentences.

Dictation   Direct students' attention to the bottom of the page and say:

Listen to this sentence: **I will tie a tight knot.** *Write the words on the line.*

Listen for It

Focus　The letters **ie** and **igh** can have the **long i** sound.

long i	
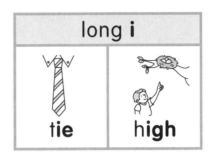 t**ie**	h**igh**

Say the picture name. Read the word.
Then underline the letters that stand for the **long i** sound.

1. pie	2. light	3. fight
4. high	5.  lie	6. thigh
7. fried	8. night	9. cries

Dictation •

1. __igh__　　2. ____ie__　　3. ____igh__

Write It

Word Box

night	tie	tried	light
fried	thigh	high	pie
bright	lie	cries	right

Read each word. Then write it under **ie** or **igh**.

ie	igh
_____	_____
_____	_____
_____	_____
_____	_____
_____	_____
_____	_____

Dictation

1. ___ ___ie___   2. ___igh___   3. ___ ___igh___

Write It

Word Box

cries	fight	fried
night	high	light
lie	thigh	pie

Write the word that names the picture.
Then circle the letters that stand for the **long i** sound.

1.

_____

2.

_____

3.

_____

4.

_____

5.

_____

6.

_____

7.

_____

8.

_____

9.

_____

Dictation

1. ___ ___ie___   2. ___igh___   3. ___igh___

Read It

Say the picture name.
Then fill in the circle next to the word that names the picture.

1. ○ fries　○ flies	**2.** ○ night　○ tight	**3.** ○ right　○ night
4.  ○ tries　○ spies	**5.** ○ dries　○ cries	**6.** ○ tights　○ lights
7. ○ thigh　○ high	**8.** ○ tied　○ tried	**9.** ○ bright　○ fright
10.  ○ lie　○ tie	**11.**  ○ sight　○ light	**12.**  ○ fried　○ cried

Dictation ···

1. ___ ___ie___　　2. ___ ___ie___　　3. ___ ___igh___

Read It

Write the words that complete the sentence.
Then read the sentence out loud.

1.

   | bright | light | sight |

   My desk _____ is too _____.

2.

   | tried | cried | spies |

   The _____ _____ to catch the thief.

3.

   | fried | fries | flies |

   Keep the _____ away from my _____!

4.

   | right | tie | night |

   What is the _____ way to _____ a knot?

5.

   | tights | sunlight | cried | dried |

   I _____ my _____ in the _____.

Dictation

· ·

_____

DAY 1 **Listening for Long o**

Read aloud the focus statement. Then point to the first example and say: *The letters* **o** *and* **a** *together in a word usually stand for the* **long o** *sound: /ō/. You hear /ō/ in* **toad***. Say* **toad***.* (toad) Repeat this process for the letters **o** and **e** in **doe**. Then read the directions and call students' attention to number 1. Say: *Point to the road. Say* **road***.* (road) *Do you hear /ō/ in* **road***?* (yes) *What letters stand for the sound of /ō/ in* **road***?* (oa) *Underline the* **o** *and* **a** *in* **road***.* Repeat this process for the remaining words.

Dictation   Direct students' attention to the bottom of the page and say:

Listen to each word I say. Then write the missing letters to complete the word.   1. load   2. foe   3. soak

DAY 2 **Listening for Long o**

Read aloud the focus statement. Then point to the example and say: *The letters* **o** *and* **w** *together in a word often stand for the* **long o** *sound: /ō/. You hear /ō/ in* **crow***. Say* **crow***.* (crow) Then read the directions and call students' attention to number 1. Say: *The first picture shows a boy mowing the lawn. Say* **mow***.* (mow) *Do you hear /ō/ in* **mow***?* (yes) *What letters stand for /ō/ in the word* **mow***?* (ow) *Underline the* **o** *and* **w** *in* **mow***.* Repeat this process for the remaining words. For number 2, be sure to point out that **tow** is a homophone of **toe**—the words sound alike but they are spelled differently and have different meanings.

Dictation   Direct students' attention to the bottom of the page and say:

Listen to each word I say. Then write the missing letter or letters to complete the word.
1. glow   2. slow   3. blow   4. show

DAY 3 **Writing Words with Long o Digraphs**

Call students' attention to the word box at the top of the page. Have students read each word aloud. Then read the directions and call students' attention to number 1. Say: *The picture shows a loaf of bread. Say* **loaf***.* (loaf) *Find the word* **loaf** *in the word box. How is* **loaf** *spelled?* (l-o-a-f) *Write the word* **loaf** *on the line under the picture. Circle the letters that have the* **long o** *sound.* Repeat this process for the remaining pictures.

Picture Key: 1. loaf, 2. row, 3. coach, 4. toes, 5. throw, 6. bowl, 7. rainbow, 8. soap, 9. float

Dictation   Direct students' attention to the bottom of the page and say:

Listen to each word I say. Then write the missing letters to complete the word.
1. goes   2. goat   3. crow   4. flown

DAY 4 **Reading Words with Long o Digraphs**

Read the directions and call students' attention to number 1. Say: *Let's read the phrase together:* **a toe with a bow***. Which words have the* **long o** *sound?* (toe, bow) *Underline the words* **toe** *and* **bow***. Then draw a line from the phrase to the correct picture.* Repeat this process for the remaining phrases.

Dictation   Direct students' attention to the bottom of the page and say:

Listen to each word I say. Then write the word on the line.   1. row   2. throw   3. soap   4. goes

DAY 5 **Reading Words with Long o Digraphs**

Read the directions and call students' attention to number 1. Say: *Let's read the incomplete sentence together:* **Do you _____ how to row a boat?** *Now let's read the two word choices:* **knot, know***. Which word completes the sentence?* (know) *Write the word* **know** *on the line.* After students finish writing, say: *Now let's read the sentence together:* **Do you know how to row a boat?** Repeat this process for the remaining sentences.

Dictation   Direct students' attention to the bottom of the page and say:

Listen to this sentence: **The goat is next to the window.** *Write the words on the line.*

Listen for It

Focus — The vowel pairs **oa** and **oe** are digraphs that usually have the **long o** sound.

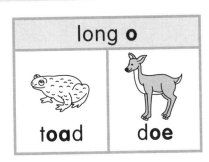

long **o**

t**oa**d	d**oe**

Say the picture name. Read the word.
Then underline the two vowels that stand for the **long o** sound.

1. road	2. toe	3.  loaf
4. soap	5. hoe	6. foam
7. coach	8.  boat	9. toast

Dictation •

1. ___oa___   2. ___oe   3. ___oa___

Skill: Listening for **long o** digraphs   **113**

Listen for It

Focus   The letter pair **ow** is a digraph that can have the **long o** sound.

long **o**

cr**ow**

Say the picture name. Read the word.
Then underline the two letters that stand for the **long o** sound.

1. mow	2.  tow	3.  row
4. crow	5.  throw	6. window
7. bowl	8. snow	9.  grown

Dictation ···

1. g___ow   2. ___ ___ow   3. ___ ___ow   4. ___ ___ow

Write It

Say the picture name. Write the word on the line.
Then circle the letters that have the **long o** sound.

1.

_____

2.

_____

3.

_____

4.

_____

5.

_____

6.

_____

7.

_____

8.

_____

9.

_____

Dictation •

1. ___oe___   2. ___oa___   3. ___ ___ow   4. ___ ___ow___

Skill: Writing words with **long o** digraphs   **115**

Read It

Read the phrase. Underline the words that have the **long o** sound.
Then draw a line from the words to the correct picture.

1. a toe with a bow

2. a goat on a road

3. a coach who mows

4. a toad that croaks

5. blowing snow

6. a coat to loan

7. a bowl of oats

Dictation ●●●

1. _____ 2. _____ 3. _____ 4. _____

Read It

Write the word that completes the sentence.
Then read the sentence out loud.

1. Do you _____ how to row a boat?

   knot   know

2. Joe knows how to _____ a baseball.

   throw   throat

3. Goats eat on the hill _____ our home.

   window   below

4. A doe was next to the old _____ tree.

   oak   boat

5. Please show me how to _____.

   float   flown

6. I will _____ you my yellow coat.

   load   loan

Dictation •

_____

Long Vowel Digraphs
ew, ue

DAY 1

Listening for Long u

Read aloud the focus statement. Then point to the first example word and say: *The letters **e** and **w** together in a word usually stand for the **long u** sound: /ū/. You hear /ū/ in **new**. Say **new**.* (new) Repeat this process for the letters **u** and **e** in **clue**. Then read the directions and call students' attention to number 1. Say: *The picture shows a gas pump. Gas is called **fuel**. Say **fuel**.* (fuel) *Do you hear /ū/ in **fuel**?* (yes) *What letters in **fuel** have the /ū/ sound?* (ue) *Underline the **u** and **e** in **fuel**.* Repeat this process for the remaining pictures.

Dictation   Direct students' attention to the bottom of the page and say:
Listen to each word I say. Then write the missing letters to complete the word.
1. news   2. drew   3. true   4. glue

DAY 2

Writing Words with Long u Digraphs

Read the directions and call students' attention to the word box. Have students read each word aloud. Then say: *Now point to the first word again. What does it say?* (flew) *Which letters have the /ū/ sound in **flew**?* (ew) *Write the word **flew** on the line in the box that says **ew** at the top.* Repeat this process for the remaining words.

Dictation   Direct students' attention to the bottom of the page and say:
Listen to each word I say. Then write the missing letters to complete the word.
1. crew   2. blue   3. brew   4. due

DAY 3

Writing Words with Long u Digraphs

Call students' attention to the word box at the top of the page. Have students read each word aloud. Then read the directions and call students' attention to number 1. Say: *The picture shows a pot of stew. Say **stew**.* (stew) *Find the word **stew** in the word box. How is **stew** spelled?* (s-t-e-w) *Write the word **stew** on the line under the picture. Circle the letters that have the **long u** sound.* Repeat this process for the remaining pictures.
Picture Key: 1. stew, 2. glue, 3. jewel, 4. fuel, 5. blew, 6. grew, 7. Tuesday, 8. threw, 9. blue

Dictation   Direct students' attention to the bottom of the page and say:
Listen to each word I say. Then write the word on the line.   1. drew   2. flew   3. clue

DAY 4

Reading Words with Long u Digraphs

Read the directions and call students' attention to number 1. Say: *Let's read the phrase together: **true blue**. Which words have the **long u** sound?* (true, blue) *Underline the words **true** and **blue**. Then draw a line from the phrase to the correct picture.* Repeat this process for the remaining phrases.

Dictation   Direct students' attention to the bottom of the page and say:
Listen to the words I say. Then write the words on the line.   1. a blue jewel   2. a new clue

DAY 5

Reading Words with Long u Digraphs

Read the directions and call students' attention to number 1. Say: *Let's read the incomplete sentence together: **Dad made _____ in the _____ pot.** Now let's read the word choices: **new, flew, stew**. Which word belongs on the first line?* (stew) *Write **stew** on the line. Which word belongs on the second line?* (new) *Write the word **new** to complete the sentence.* After students finish writing, say: *Now let's read the sentence together: **Dad made stew in the new pot.*** Repeat this process for the remaining sentences.

Dictation   Direct students' attention to the bottom of the page and say:
*Listen to this sentence: **I have a new blue coat.** Write the words on the line.*

Name _____

Listen for It

Focus The letter pairs **ew** and **ue** are digraphs that usually have the **long u** sound.

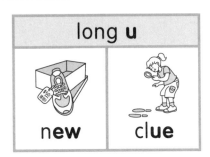

long u
new	clue

Say the picture name. Read the word.
Then underline the two letters that stand for the **long u** sound.

1. fuel	2. flew	3. chew
4. blue	5. grew	6. glue
7. Sue	8. jewel	9. Tuesday

Dictation •

1. ___ew___   2. ___ ___ew   3. ___ ___ue   4. ___ ___ue

Write It

Word Box

flew	grew	clue	Tuesday
stew	blue	hue	chew
glue	due	screw	jewel

Read each word. Then write it under the correct letter pair.

ew	ue
_____	_____
_____	_____
_____	_____
_____	_____
_____	_____
_____	_____

Dictation

1. ____ ____ew   2. ____ ____ue   3. ____ ____ew   4. ____ue

Write It

Word Box

blew	blue	fuel
glue	grew	jewel
stew	threw	Tuesday

Say the picture name. Write the word on the line.
Then circle the letters that have the **long u** sound.

1.

_____

2.

_____

3.

_____

4.

_____

5.

_____

6.

_____

7.

_____

8.

_____

9.

_____

Dictation

1. _____   2. _____   3. _____

Skill: Writing words with **long u** digraphs

Read It

Read each phrase. Underline the word or words that have the **long u** sound.
Then draw a line to the correct picture.

1. true blue

2. a bone to chew

3. fuel for a car

4. a pot of stew

5. a jewel on a ring

6. a few screws

7. a plant that grew

Dictation

1. _____   2. _____

Read It

Write the words that complete the sentence.
Then read the sentence out loud.

1.

   new   flew   stew

   Dad made _____ in the _____ pot.

2.

   glue   blue   drew

   I _____ with puffy _____.

3.

   few   news   chews

   Buddy _____ a _____ bones each day.

4.

   fuel   true   news

   The _____ about Sue is _____.

5.

   threw   true   screws

   Mom _____ the _____ into the bag.

Dictation ···

_____

Short Vowel Digraphs
ea, ou

DAY 1

Listening for Short e

Read aloud the focus statement. Then say: *Usually the letters **e** and **a** together in a word have the **long e** sound you hear in **bean**. Today we are going to read words with **ea** that have the **short e** sound /ĕ/ as in **head**. Point to your head and say **head**.* (head) *Now say /ĕ/.* (/ĕ/) Then read the directions and call students' attention to number 1. Say: *Point to the bread. Say **bread**.* (bread) *Do you hear /ĕ/ in **bread**?* (yes) *Fill in the circle next to **yes**.* Repeat this process for the remaining words.

Dictation   Direct students' attention to the bottom of the page and say:

Listen to each word I say. Then write the missing letters to complete the word.   1. head   2. heavy   3. dead

DAY 2

Writing Words with Short e Digraphs: ea

Direct students' attention to the word box and have them read the words aloud. Point out that the word **read** has the /ē/ sound when it is in the present tense and the /ĕ/ sound when it is in the past tense. Then read the directions and call students' attention to number 1. Say: *Let's read this sentence together: **Your brain is inside your _____.** Which word completes the sentence?* (head) *Write the word **head** on the line.* After students finish writing, say: *Now let's read the sentence together: **Your brain is inside your head.*** Repeat this process for the remaining sentences. For the word **wheat** in number 2, model how to decode unfamiliar words spelled with **ea** by reading **wheat** with a **short e** sound and then with a **long e** sound to see which pronunciation stands for a familiar word. For the word **read** in number 4, point out that the phrase "last week" means that the action happened in the past, so the word **read** should be pronounced /rĕd/ not /rēd/.

Dictation   Direct students' attention to the bottom of the page and say:

Listen to each word I say. Then write the word you hear.
1. read (as in "I read a book yesterday.")   2. ready   3. bread

DAY 3

Listening for Short u

Read aloud the focus statement. Then point to the example and say: *The letters **o** and **u** together in a word can have the /ŭ/ sound you hear in **touch**, as in "Touch your toes." Say **touch**.* (touch) Then read the directions and call students' attention to number 1. Say: *Point to the young child. Say **young**.* (young) *Do you hear /ŭ/ in **young**?* (yes) *Fill in the circle next to **yes**. Which letters in **young** have the **short u** sound?* (ou) Repeat this process for the remaining words.

Dictation   Direct students' attention to the bottom of the page and say:

Listen to each word I say. Then write the missing letters to complete the word.   1. touch   2. young   3. tough

DAY 4

Writing Words with Short u Digraphs: ou

Direct students' attention to the word box at the top of the page. Have them read the words aloud. Then read the directions and call students' attention to number 1. Say: *Let's read this sentence together: **A brick wall feels _____.** Which word best completes the sentence?* (rough) *Write the word **rough** on the line.* After students finish writing, say: *Now let's read the sentence together: **A brick wall feels rough.*** Repeat this process for the remaining sentences.

Dictation   Direct students' attention to the bottom of the page and say:

Listen to each word I say. Write the word you hear.   1. rough   2. enough   3. touch

DAY 5

Reading Words with Short Vowel Digraphs: ea, ou

Read the directions and call students' attention to number 1. Say: *Let's read the sentence: **The meat in this stew is too _____ to chew.** Now let's read the two word choices: **enough, tough**. Which word completes the sentence?* (tough) *Write **tough** on the line.* After students finish writing, say: *Now let's read the sentence together: **The meat in this stew is too tough to chew.*** Repeat this process for the remaining sentences.

Dictation   Direct students' attention to the bottom of the page and say:

*Listen to this sentence: **I have had enough bread.** Write the words on the line.*

Listen for It

Focus The vowel digraph **ea** sometimes has the **short e** sound.

short e

head

Say the picture name. Then read the word.
Does it have the **short e** sound? Fill in the circle next to **yes** or **no**.

1. bread
   ○ yes   no

2. seal
   yes   ○ no

3. feather
   ○ yes   no

4. spread
   ○ yes   ○ no

5. sweat
   ○ yes   ○ no

6. peach
   ○ yes   ○ no

7. bean
   yes   ○ no

8. thread
   ○ yes   ○ no

9. sweater
   ○ yes   no

Dictation •

1. ___ea___   2. ___ea___ ___   3. ___ea___

Name _____

Write It

Word Box

sweat	bread	head
read	ready	sweater

Write the word that completes the sentence.

1.  Your brain is inside your _____.

2.  Do you like to eat wheat _____?

3.  The hot sun makes me _____.

4.  I _____ five books last week.

5.  My _____ is too tight for me.

6.  Kate is _____ to bake a cake.

Dictation

1. _____   2. _____   3. _____

Skill: Writing words with **short e** digraphs   Daily Phonics • EMC 2789 • © Evan-Moor Corp.

Listen for It

Focus   The vowel pair **ou** is a digraph that can have the **short u** sound.

short **u**

t**ou**ch

Read the word. Does it have the **short u** sound?
Fill in the circle next to **yes** or **no**.

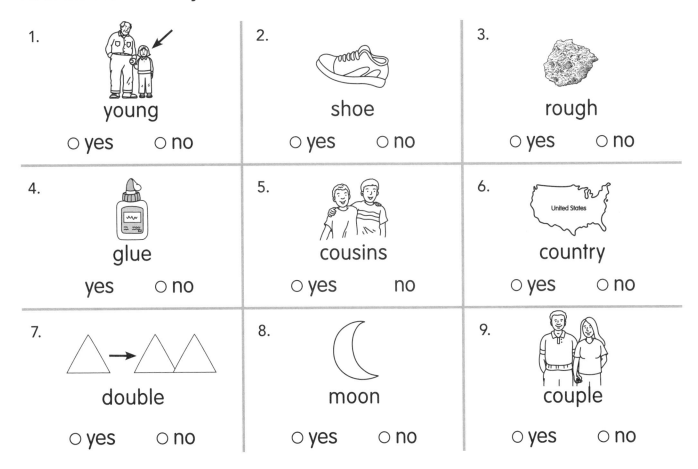

1. young   ○ yes   ○ no

2. shoe   ○ yes   ○ no

3. rough   ○ yes   ○ no

4. glue   yes   ○ no

5. cousins   ○ yes   no

6. country   ○ yes   ○ no

7. double   ○ yes   ○ no

8. moon   ○ yes   ○ no

9. couple   ○ yes   ○ no

Dictation ....

1. ___ou_____   2. ___ou_____   3. ___ou_____

Write It

Word Box

country	cousin	enough
rough	touch	young

Write the word that completes the sentence.

1. A brick wall feels _____.

2. I live in a very large _____.

3. I am _____, but Gramps is not.

4. My cat is soft to _____.

5. You must try to get _____ sleep.

6. My _____ and I are the same age.

Dictation

1. _____   2. _____   3. _____

Read It

Write the word that completes the sentence.
Then read the sentence out loud.

1. The meat in this stew is too _____ to chew.
   enough   tough

2. Joe is _____ in the race.
   ahead   head

3. If you _____ the hot stove, you will be in trouble!
   tough   touch

4. I have a young _____ named Doug.
   cousin   country

5. The baby bird is _____ to grow feathers.
   read   ready

6. I like to spread jam on _____.
   braid   bread

Dictation •

_____

The Sounds of oo

DAY 1 **Listening for the Sounds of oo**

Read aloud the focus statement as you point to each example. Have students say each word after you, emphasizing the /o͞o/ or /o͝o/ sound. Then read the directions and call students' attention to number 1. Say: *Point to the zoo. Do you hear /o͞o/ or /o͝o/ in **zoo**?* (/o͞o/) *Now point to the tooth. Do you hear /o͞o/ in **tooth**?* (yes) *Fill in the circle below the tooth. Now point to the book. Do you hear /o͞o/ in **book**?* (no) *Do <u>not</u> fill in the circle.* Repeat this process for the remaining pictures and rows.

Picture Key: Row 1: zoo, tooth, book, moon; Row 2: foot, cook, hook, broom; Row 3: pool, wood, boot, spoon; Row 4: cookie, hood, moose, football

Dictation Direct students' attention to the bottom of the page and say:

Listen to each word I say. Then write the word on the line. 1. spoon 2. book 3. broom

DAY 2 **Writing Words with the oo Digraph**

Direct students' attention to the word box at the top of the page. Then read the directions and call students' attention to number 1. Say: *The picture shows a cook. Say **cook**.* (cook) *Find the word **cook** in the word box. How is it spelled?* (c-o-o-k) *Write the word **cook** on the line under the picture.* Repeat this process for the remaining pictures.

Dictation Direct students' attention to the bottom of the page and say:

Listen to each word I say. Then write the word on the line. 1. boot 2. mood 3. foot 4. moon

DAY 3 **Writing Words with the oo Digraph**

Read the directions and call students' attention to the word box. Have them read the words aloud. If necessary, have students try saying each word with the /o͞o/ and then the /o͝o/ sound to decide which is correct. Then have students return to the first word. Say: *What does this word say?* (book) *Does **book** have the /o͞o/ sound you hear in **pool** or the /o͝o/ sound you hear in **wood**?* (/o͝o/ in wood) *Write the word on the line in the box that says **wood**.* Repeat this process for the remaining words.

Dictation Direct students' attention to the bottom of the page and say:

Listen to each word I say. Then write the word on the line. 1. good 2. food 3. zoom 4. hood

DAY 4 **Reading Words with the oo Digraph**

Read the directions and call students' attention to phrase number 1. Say: *Let's read number 1 together: **a moose on the loose**. Do you hear /o͞o/ or /o͝o/ in **moose**?* (/o͞o/) *Underline the word **moose**. Do you hear /o͞o/ or /o͝o/ in **loose**?* (/o͞o/) *Underline the word **loose**. Now which picture goes with **a moose on the loose**?* (the moose) *Draw a line from the words to the picture.* Repeat this process for the remaining phrases.

Dictation Direct students' attention to the bottom of the page and say:

*Listen to this sentence: **The foot of a moose is called a hoof.** Now write the missing words: **foot, moose, hoof.***

DAY 5 **Reading Words with the oo Digraph**

Read the directions and call students' attention to number 1. Say: *Let's read the sentence together: **The _____ is made of _____**. Now let's read the word choices: **wood, cook, spoon**. Which word belongs on the first line?* (spoon) *Write **spoon** on the line. Which word belongs on the second line?* (wood) *Write the word **wood** to complete the sentence.* After students finish writing, say: *Let's read the sentence together: **The spoon is made of wood.*** Repeat this process for the remaining sentences.

Dictation Direct students' attention to the bottom of the page and say:

*Listen to this sentence: **I read a good book about the moon.** Write the words on the line.*

Listen for It

Focus The vowel pair **oo** is a digraph that can have the sound you hear in **boot**. It can also have the sound you hear in **hook**.

b**oo**t   h**oo**k

Say the picture name. Listen to the vowel sound. Then name each picture in the row. Fill in the circle if it has the same vowel sound as the first picture.

1.

○   ○   ○

2.

○   ○   ○   ○

3.

○   ○   ○

4.

○   ○   ○

Dictation •

1. _____   2. _____   3. _____

Write It

Word Box

brook	cook	food
goose	hood	root
spoon	tooth	zoo

Say the picture name.
Write the word on the line.

1.

_____

2.

_____

3.

_____

4.

_____

5.

_____

6.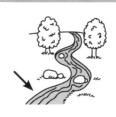

_____

7.

_____

8.

_____

9.

_____

Dictation

1. _____   2. _____   3. _____   4. _____

Write It

Word Box

book	cool	football	good	moon
pool	snoop	stood	shoot	wood

Read each word in the box above.
Then write it under the word in bold type that has the same **oo** sound.

long	short
pool	**wood**
_____	_____
_____	_____
_____	_____
_____	_____
_____	_____

Dictation •

1. _____   2. _____   3. _____   4. _____

Name _____

Read It

Read the phrase. Underline the words that have the vowel sound in **broom**.
Circle the words that have the vowel sound in **wood**.
Then draw a line to the correct picture.

1. a **moose** on the **loose**

2. **spoons** for the **cook**

3. a deep **pool**

4. a **good book**

5. the yellow **moon**

6. a pile of **wood**

Dictation

The _____ of a _____ is called a _____.

Read It

Write the words that complete the sentence.
Then read the sentence out loud.

1.

wood   cook   spoon

The _____ is made of _____.

2.

zoo   goose   moose

The _____ flew into the _____.

3.

cool   fool   pool

I need to _____ off in the _____.

4.

foot   mood   boot

That _____ is too big for my _____.

5.

room   boom   broom

I need a _____ to sweep my _____.

Dictation •••

_____

Variant Vowel Digraphs
au, aw

DAY 1
Listening for Digraphs: au, aw
Read aloud the focus statement as you point to each example. Have students say each word after you, emphasizing the /aw/ sound. Then read the directions and call students' attention to number 1. Say: *Point to the paws. Say* **paws**. (paws) *Which letters in* **paws** *have the /aw/ sound?* (aw) *Underline the* **aw** *in* **paws**. Repeat this process for the remaining words.

Dictation Direct students' attention to the bottom of the page and say:
Listen to each word I say. Then write the letters that stand for the sounds you hear.
1. fault   2. lawn   3. haul   4. draw

DAY 2
Writing Words with the /aw/ Sound
Read the directions and call students' attention to the word box. Say: *Point to the first word. What does it say?* (pause) *This word means "to stop for a moment." Which letters have the /aw/ sound in* **pause**? (au) *Write the word on the line in the box that says* **au**. After students finish writing, say: *Now find the other word in the word box that says /pawz/. How is it spelled?* (p-a-w-s) *Do you know what this word means?* (an animal's feet) *Which letters have the /aw/ sound in* **paws**? (aw) *Write the word on the line in the box that says* **aw**. Repeat this process for the remaining words.

Dictation Direct students' attention to the bottom of the page and say:
Listen to each word I say. Then write the letters that stand for the sounds you hear.
1. dawn   2. fault   3. vault   4. straw

DAY 3
Writing Words with Digraphs: au, aw
Read the directions and call students' attention to the word box at the top of the page. Have students read the words aloud. Then call their attention to number 1. Say: *Point to the claw. Listen to the letter-sounds as you say* **claw**. (/k/ /l/ /aw/) *Find* **claw** *in the word box and write the word on the line. Which letters in the word* **claw** *stand for /aw/?* (aw) *Circle the* **a** *and* **w** *in* **claw**. Repeat this process for the remaining words.
Picture Key: 1. claw, 2. hawk, 3. paws, 4. vault, 5. jaw, 6. haunt, 7. fawn, 8. faucet, 9. draw

Dictation Direct students' attention to the bottom of the page and say:
Listen to this sentence: **A hawk sat on the seesaw.** *Write the words on the line.*

DAY 4
Reading Words with Digraphs: au, aw
Read the directions and call students' attention to phrase number 1. Say: *Let's read number 1 together:* **a big yawn**. *Which letters in the word* **yawn** *have the /aw/ sound?* (aw) *Underline the* **a** *and* **w** *in* **yawn**. *Then draw a line from the phrase to the correct picture.* Repeat this process for the remaining phrases.

Dictation Direct students' attention to the bottom of the page and say:
Listen to this sentence: **I have sauce on my jaw.** *Write the words on the line.*

DAY 5
Reading Words with Digraphs: au, aw
Read the directions and call students' attention to number 1. Say: *Let's read the incomplete sentence together:* **I saw a _____ and a doe on our lawn.** *Now let's read the word choices:* **fun, fawn**. *Which word belongs on the line?* (fawn) *Write* **fawn** *on the line.* After students finish writing, say: *Now let's read the sentence together:* **I saw a fawn and a doe on our lawn.** Repeat this process for the remaining sentences.

Dictation Direct students' attention to the bottom of the page and say:
Listen to this sentence: **We have a seesaw on our lawn.** *Write the words on the line.*

Listen for It

Focus The letter pairs **au** and **aw** are digraphs that can have the vowel sound you hear in **haul** and **claw**.

haul    claw

Say the picture name. Read the word.
Then underline the letters that stand for the vowel sound you hear in **raw**.

1. 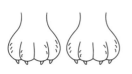 paws	2. hawk	3. sauce
4.  caught	5. yawn	6. August
7.  straw	8.  faucet	9.  seesaw

Dictation •

1. ___au___ ___   2. ___aw___   3. ___au___   4. ___ ___aw

Write It

Word Box

pause	straw	fawn	haunt	fault
faucet	jaw	paws	draw	sauce

Read each word in the box above.

Then write the word under the correct letter pair.

au	aw
_____	_____
_____	_____
_____	_____
_____	_____
_____	_____

Dictation •

1. ___aw___   2. ___au_____   3. ___au_____   4. _____aw

Write It

Word Box

claw	draw	faucet
fawn	haunt	jaw
hawk	paws	vault

Say the picture name. Write the word on the line.
Then circle the letters that stand for the **/aw/** sound.

1.

_____

2.

_____

3.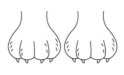

_____

4.

_____

5.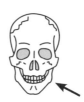

_____

6.

_____

7.

_____

8.

_____

9.

_____

Dictation

_____

Skill: Writing words with the **/aw/** sound **139**

Read It

Read the phrase. Underline the letters that have the /aw/ sound.
Then draw a line from the words to the correct picture.

1. a big **yawn**

2. a **lawn** with a path

3. **paws** with **claws**

4. a bank **vault**

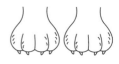

5. a bent **straw**

6. **sauce** to eat

7. a **hawk** that **squawks**

8. a cup and **saucer**

Dictation •

_____

Read It

Write the word that completes the sentence.
Then read the sentence out loud.

1. I saw a _____ and a doe on our lawn.
   fun   fawn

2. A hawk grabs food with its _____.
   clues   claws

3. The truck will _____ the pile of straw away.
   haul   hole

4. We will _____ the rocket at dawn.
   launch   lunch

5. What caused you to _____ in class?
   haul   yawn

6. My cat will lick his _____.
   peas   paws

Dictation ···

_____

Diphthongs
ou, ow, oi, oy

DAY 1

Listening for the /ou/ Sound

Read aloud the focus statement as you point to each example. Have students repeat each word after you, emphasizing the /ou/ sound. Then read the directions and call students' attention to number 1. Say: *This person is taking a bow. Say **bow**.* (bow) *What vowel sound do you hear in **bow**?* (/ou/) Remind students that the letter pair **ow** can also have the **long o** sound as in the word **bow**, meaning something you tie. Then ask: *Which letters in **bow** have the /ou/ sound?* (ow) *Circle the **o** and **w** in **bow**.* Repeat this process for the remaining words. For numbers 5 and 6, point out that the words **flour** and **flower** are homophones.

Dictation   Direct students' attention to the bottom of the page and say:

Listen to each word I say. Then write the missing letters to complete the word.
1. loud   2. shout   3. town   3. frown

DAY 2

Writing Words with the /ou/ Sound

Read the directions and call students' attention to number 1. Say: *The picture shows a bag of flour. Say **flour**.* (flour) *Look at the word box at the top of the page and find the word **flour**. How is it spelled?* (f-l-o-u-r) *Write it on the line under the picture. Then circle the letters that have the /ou/ sound.* Repeat this process for the remaining pictures.

Picture Key: 1. flour, 2. down, 3. cloud, 4. tower, 5. mouth, 6. couch, 7. frown, 8. crowd, 9. scout

Dictation   Direct students' attention to the bottom of the page and say:

Listen to each word I say. Then write the missing letters to complete the word.
1. pound   2. south   3. brow   4. gown

DAY 3

Listening for the /oi/ Sound

Read aloud the focus statement as you point to each example. Have students repeat each word after you, emphasizing the /oi/ sound. Then read the directions and call students' attention to number 1. Say: *Point to the boy. Say **boy**.* (boy) *What vowel sound do you hear in **boy**?* (/oi/) *Which letters in **boy** have the /oi/ sound?* (oy) *Underline the **o** and **y** in **boy**.* Repeat this process for the remaining words.

Dictation   Direct students' attention to the bottom of the page and say:

Listen to each word I say. Then write the word you hear.   *1. join   2. joy   3. cowboy*

DAY 4

Writing Words with the /oi/ Sound

Direct students' attention to the word box at the top of the page. Have them read the words aloud. Then read the directions and call students' attention to number 1. Say: *Let's read the clue: **round money**. What kind of money is round?* (coin) *Look at the word box at the top of the page and find the word **coins**. How is it spelled?* (c-o-i-n-s) *Write **coins** on the line.* Repeat this process for the remaining clues.

Dictation   Direct students' attention to the bottom of the page and say:

*Listen to this sentence: **Do not get soil on the toy.** Write the words on the line.*

DAY 5

Reading Words with /ou/ and /oi/ Sounds

Read the directions and call students' attention to number 1. Say: *Let's read the incomplete sentence: **You can mix the wheat _____ with the _____.** Now let's read the word choices together: oil, boil, flour. Which word belongs on the first line?* (flour) *Write **flour** on the line. Which word belongs on the second line?* (oil) *Write the word **oil** to complete the sentence.* After students finish writing, say: *Let's read the sentence together: **You can mix the wheat flour with the oil.*** Repeat this process for the remaining sentences.

Dictation   Direct students' attention to the bottom of the page and say:

*Listen to this sentence: **The cowboy gave me a coin.** Write the words on the line.*

Name _____

Listen for It

Focus The letter pairs **ou** and **ow** sometimes have the vowel sound you hear in **cloud** and in **clown**.

cloud  clown

Say the picture name. Then read the word.
Circle the letters that stand for the vowel sound you hear in **how**.

1.  bow	2. mouse	3. gown
4. crown	5.  flour	6. flower
7. mouth	8. couch	9.  owl

Dictation •

1. ___ou___   2. ___ ___ou___   3. ___ow___   4. ___ ___ow___

Skill: Listening for the /ou/ sound   **143**

Write It

Word Box

cloud	couch	crowd
down	flour	frown
mouth	scout	tower

Say the picture name. Write the word on the line.
Then circle the letters that have the vowel sound you hear in **clown**.

1.

_____

2.

_____

3.

_____

4.

_____

5.

_____

6.

_____

7.

_____

8.

_____

9.

_____

Dictation

1. ___ou___   2. ___ou___   3. _____ow___   4. ___ow___

Listen for It

The letter pairs **oi** and **oy** have the vowel sound you hear in **coins** and in **toy**. The letter pair **oi** usually comes in the middle of a word. The letter pair **oy** usually comes at the end of a word.

| coins | | toy | |

Say the picture name. Then read the word.
Underline the letters that stand for the vowel sound you hear in **boy**.

1. boy	2. coin	3.  oil
4.  joy	5. cowboy	6. soil
7. coil	8.  toys	9. point

Dictation ···

1. _____   2. _____   3. _____

Write It

Word Box

toys	boil	coins	cowboy
coil	point	joy	soil

Read the clue. Then write the correct word on the line.

1. round money _____

2. a man on a ranch _____

3. a place for a plant _____

4. to show where to go _____

5. to go around and around _____

6. a way to cook _____

7. fun to play with _____

8. a happy feeling _____

Dictation

_____

Read It

Write the words that complete the sentence.
Then read the sentence out loud.

1. oil   boil   flour

    You can mix the wheat _____ with the _____.

2. gown   clown   toy

    The _____ gave Roy a funny _____.

3. soil   flowers   soy

    Will _____ grow in this rocky _____?

4. joy   join   scout

    I will _____ a _____ troop in the fall.

5. mouse   town   couch

    Did you see a _____ run under the _____?

Dictation •

_____

R-Controlled Vowels
ar, or, er, ir, ur

DAY 1

Listening for R-Controlled Vowels: ar, or

Read aloud the focus statement. Then point to the first example and say: *The letters **a** and **r** together can have this sound: /ar/. Say /ar/. You hear /ar/ in **barn**. Say **barn**.* (barn) *The letters **o** and **r** blend together to have this sound: /or/. Say /or/. (/or/) You hear /or/ in **corn**. Say **corn**.* (corn) *Then read the directions and call students' attention to number 1. Say: Point to the boy's arm. Say **arm**.* (arm) *What **vowel** + **r** sound do you hear in **arm**?* (/ar/) *What letters stand for that sound?* (ar) *Fill in the circle next to the letters **ar**. Repeat this process for the remaining pictures.*

Picture Key: 1. arm, 2. horse, 3. fork, 4. yarn, 5. park, 6. stork, 7. forty, 8. shark, 9. card

Dictation Direct students' attention to the bottom of the page and say:
Listen to each word I say. Then write the word you hear.   1. arm   2. yarn   3. fork   4. stork

DAY 2

Writing R-Controlled Vowels: ar, or

Call students' attention to the letter box and review the sound that each letter pair stands for. Then read the directions and call students' attention to number 1. Say: *Point to the card. Say **card**.* (card) *What **vowel** + **r** sound do you hear in **card**?* (/ar/) *Which letters stand for /ar/?* (ar) *Write the letters **a** and **r** on the lines to spell the word **card**. After students finish writing, say: Now let's read the word together: **card**. Repeat this process for the remaining words.*

Dictation Direct students' attention to the bottom of the page and say:
Listen to each word I say. Then write the word you hear.   1. farm   2. form   3. pork   4. park

DAY 3

Listening for R-Controlled Vowels: er, ir, ur

Read aloud the focus statement. Then point to the first example and say: *The letter pair **er** has the /ur/ sound you hear in **person**. Say /ur/. (ur) Say **person**.* (person) *Repeat this process for **ir** and **ur**. Then read the directions and call students' attention to number 1. Say: Point to the girl. Say **girl**.* (girl) *What **vowel** + **r** sound do you hear in **girl**?* (/ur/) *Which letters stand for the /ur/ sound in **girl**?* (ir) *Underline the letters **i** and **r** in **girl**. Repeat this process for the remaining words.*

Dictation Direct students' attention to the bottom of the page and say:
Listen to each word I say. Then write the missing letters to complete the word.   1. surf   2. verb   3. dirt

DAY 4

Writing Words with R-Controlled Vowels: er, ir, ur

Read the directions and call students' attention to the word box. Have them read each word aloud and underline the two letters that have the /ur/ sound. Then say: *Look at number 1. Let's read the definition together: **below**. Which word from the word box means "below"?* (under) *Write the word **under** on the line. Repeat this process for the remaining definitions.*

Dictation Direct students' attention to the bottom of the page and say:
Listen to each word I say. Then write the missing letters to complete the word.   1. burn   2. river   3. first

DAY 5

Reading Words with R-Controlled Vowels: ar, or, er, ir, ur

Read the directions and call students' attention to number 1. Say: *Let's read the incomplete sentence together: **The _____ lit up the dark sky**. Now let's read the word choices together: **stars, stirs**. Which word belongs on the line?* (stars) *Write **stars** on the line. After students finish writing, say: Now let's read the sentence together: **The stars lit up the dark sky**. Repeat this process for the remaining sentences.*

Dictation Direct students' attention to the bottom of the page and say:
*Listen to this sentence: **The corn in the barn is dirty**. Now write the words on the line.*

Listen for It

Focus When a vowel is followed by the letter **r**, the **r** changes the sound of the vowel. The sounds blend to make a new sound.

ar		or	
b**ar**n		c**or**n	

Say the picture name. Fill in the circle next to the letters that stand for the **vowel + r** sound you hear.

1.  ○ ar ○ or

2.  ○ ar ○ or

3.   ○ ar ○ or

4.   ○ ar ○ or

5.  ○ ar ○ or

6.   ○ ar ○ or

7.  ○ ar ○ or

8.  ○ ar ○ or

9.   ○ ar ○ or

Dictation ....

1. _____   2. _____   3. _____   4. _____

Write It

Letter Box

ar   or

Say the picture name.
Then write the missing letters to spell the word.

1.  c ___ ___ d	2. f ___ ___ k	3. b ___ ___ n
4.  p ___ ___ k	5. c ___ ___ n	6. h ___ ___ n
7.  m ___ ___ ch	8.  st ___ ___ m	9.  p ___ ___ ty

Dictation

1. _____   2. _____   3. _____   4. _____

Listen for It

Focus When an **e**, an **i**, or a **u** is followed by an **r**, the vowel sound blends with the **r** to make a new sound. The letter pairs **er**, **ir**, and **ur** have the same sound you hear in **fur**.

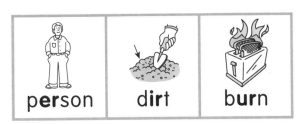

person   dirt   burn

Say the picture name. Then read the word.
Underline the letters that have the **vowel + r** sound you hear in **fur**.

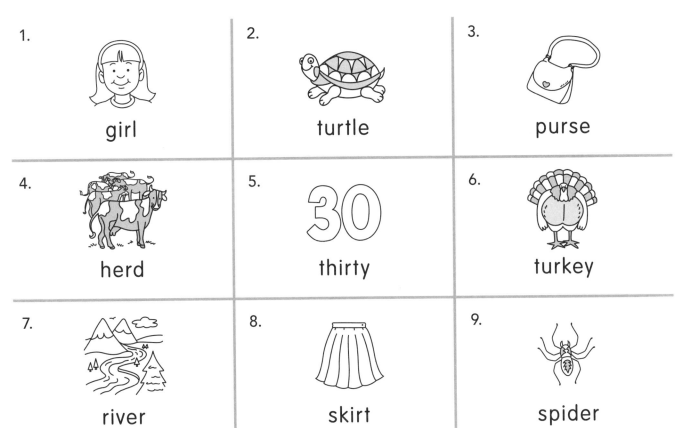

1. girl

2. turtle

3. purse

4. herd

5. thirty

6. turkey

7. river

8. skirt

9. spider

Dictation ·

1. _____ur_____   2. _____er_____   3. _____ir_____

Write It

Word Box

dirty	herd	curb	purse
spider	stir	turkey	under

Read each word in the box above. Underline the letters that stand for the **vowel + r** sound. Then read each definition below and write the word that goes with it.

1. below _____

2. to mix _____

3. a kind of bird _____

4. spins a web _____

5. not clean _____

6. a group of cows _____

7. side of the road _____

8. a bag for a lady _____

Dictation

1. ___ur___   2. _____er   3. ___ir_____

Read It

Write the word that completes the sentence.
Then read the sentence out loud.

1. The _____ lit up the dark sky.
   stars   stirs

2. The horse must stay in the _____.
   burn   barn

3. It is your _____ to feed the bird.
   turn   torn

4. What _____ do you play at the park?
   spurt   sport

5. We have a _____ of thirty cows.
   hard   herd

6. Burt is washing the _____ off his arm.
   dirt   dart

Dictation •

_____

R-Controlled Vowels
air, are, ear

DAY 1

Listening for R-Controlled Vowels: air, are

Read aloud the focus statement. Then point to the example as you say: *The letter combination **a-i-r** has the /âr/ sound you hear in **fair**. Say /âr/.* (/âr/) *Say **fair**.* (fair) Repeat this process for the **a-r-e** combination in **share**. Then read the directions and call students' attention to number 1. Say: *A female horse is called a **mare**. Say **mare**.* (mare) *Now read the word: **mare**. What vowel sound do you hear in **mare**?* (/âr/) *Which letters have the /âr/ sound?* (a-r-e) *Underline the letters **a-r-e**.* Repeat this process for the remaining words, pointing out the homophone pairs: **hair**, **hare** and **stares**, **stairs**.

Dictation   Direct students' attention to the bottom of the page and say:

Listen to each word I say. Then write the letters that stand for the sounds you hear.
1. fair   2. dare   3. upstairs   4. rare

DAY 2

Writing Words with R-Controlled Vowels: air, are

Read the directions and call students' attention to number 1. Say: *The picture shows a chair. Say **chair**.* (chair) *Look at the word box at the top of the page and find the word **chair**. How is it spelled?* (c-h-a-i-r) *Write it on the line under the picture. Then circle the letters that have the /âr/ sound.* Repeat this process for the remaining pictures.

Picture Key: 1. chair, 2. hare, 3. pair, 4. share, 5. hair, 6. mare, 7. square, 8. scare, 9. stairs

Dictation   Direct students' attention to the bottom of the page and say:

Listen to each word I say. Then write the missing letters to complete the word.   1. glare   2. airport   3. stairway

DAY 3

Listening for R-Controlled Vowels: ear

Read aloud the focus statement. Then point to the first example and have students say the word **ear**. Point to the second example and say: *The word **bear** has the /âr/ sound. Say /âr/.* (/âr/) *Say **bear**.* (bear) Then read the directions and call students' attention to number 1. Say: *Let's read the sentence together: **You hear with your ear**. Does the word **hear** have the **vowel + r** sound in **ear** or **bear**?* (ear) *Circle the word **hear**.* Repeat this process for the remaining sentences, having students circle words with the /îr/ sound and underline words with the /âr/ sound.

Dictation   Direct students' attention to the bottom of the page and say:

Listen to each word I say. Then write the letters that stand for the sounds you hear.
1. fear   2. gear   3. spear   4. swear

DAY 4

Writing Words with R-Controlled Vowels: air, are, ear

Call students' attention to the word box. Have them read each word aloud. Then read the directions and call students' attention to number 1. Say: *The picture shows a square. Say **square**.* (square) *Find the word **square** in the word box. How is **square** spelled?* (s-q-u-a-r-e) *Write the word **square** on the line under the picture.* Repeat this process for the remaining pictures.

Dictation   Direct students' attention to the bottom of the page and say:

*Listen to this sentence: **Do not stare at my hair**. Write the words on the line.*

DAY 5

Reading Words with R-Controlled Vowels: air, are, ear

Read the directions and call students' attention to number 1. Say: *Let's read the incomplete sentence together: **Clare will take _____ of the old _____**. Now let's read the word choices together: **mare, dare, care**. Which word belongs on the first line?* (care) *Write **care** on the line. Which word belongs on the second line?* (mare) *Write the word **mare** to complete the sentence.* After students finish writing, say: *Let's read the sentence together: **Clare will take care of the old mare**.* Repeat this process for the remaining sentences.

Dictation   Direct students' attention to the bottom of the page and say:

*Listen to this sentence: **I will wear my new pair of boots**. Write the words on the line.*

Name _____

Listen for It

Focus The letter combinations **air** and **are** have the **vowel + r** sound you hear in **fair**.

fair | share

Say the picture name. Read the word.
Then underline the letters that have the **r + vowel** sound you hear in **fair**.

1.

mare

2.

hair

3.

stares

4.

chair

5.

scare

6.

pair

7.

stairs

8.

hare

9.

share

Dictation ●●

1. ___ai___   2. ___are   3. _____air___   4. ___are

Write It

Word Box

hare	chair	hair
mare	pair	square
scare	share	stairs

Say the picture name. Write the word on the line.
Then circle the letters with the **vowel + r** sound.

1.

_____

2.

_____

3.

_____

4.

_____

5.

_____

6.

_____

7.

_____

8.

_____

9.

_____

Dictation

1. _____ _____ are   2. air _____ _____ _____   3. _____ _____ air _____ _____ _____

Listen for It

Focus | When the vowel pair **ea** is followed by an **r**, it often has the **vowel + r** sound you hear in **ear**. It can also have the **vowel + r** sound you hear in **bear**.

| ear | | b**ear** | |

Read the sentence. Say the word in bold type. Circle the word if it has the **vowel + r** sound in **ear**. Underline the word if it has the **vowel + r** sound in **bear**.

1. You **hear** with your ear.

2. You **wear** a sweater.

3. You eat a **pear**.

4. You cry **tears** when you are sad.

5. If you stand next to me, you stand **near**.

6. If you rip your pants, you **tear** them.

7. You see inside a **clear** glass.

8. You stay away from a **bear**.

Dictation

1. ___ear   2. ___ear   3. _____ear   4. _____ear

Write It

Word Box

bear	chair	clear
hair	fair	pear
square	stare	tears

Say the picture name. Then write the word on the line.

1.

_____

2.

_____

3.

_____

4.

_____

5.

_____

6.

_____

7.

_____

8.

_____

9.

_____

Dictation ·

_____

Read It

Write the words that complete the sentence.
Then read the sentence out loud.

1.   mare   dare   care

Clare will take _____ of the old _____.

2.   pear   share   scare

I will _____ my _____ with you.

3.   clear   care   stare

I like to _____ at the _____ blue sky.

4.   fair   stairs   chair

Please put the _____ at the top of the _____.

5.   near   pair   bear

Do not go _____ the _____ and her cubs.

Dictation ●

_____

Plural Noun Endings
s, es, ies

DAY 1

Reading Words with Plural Endings

Read aloud the focus statement. Then point to the example and say: *The first word is* **bear**. *Say* **bear**. (bear) *What is added to show more than one bear?* (s) *Yes, the plural form of* **bear** *is* **bears**. *Say* **bears**. (bears) *What sound does the* **s** *have at the end of* **bears**? (/z/) Then read the directions and call students' attention to number 1. Say: *Does the picture show one nut or more than one nut?* (more than one nut) *Read the words under the picture.* (nut, nuts) *Which word means more than one nut?* (nuts) *Fill in the circle next to the word* **nuts**. *What sound does the* **s** *have in* **nuts**? (s) Repeat this process for the remaining pictures.

Dictation   Direct students' attention to the bottom of the page and say:

Listen to each word I say. Then write the word you hear.   1. steps   2. gifts   3. flags   4. horns

DAY 2

Writing Words with Plural Endings

Read aloud the focus statement. Then point to the first example and say: *The plural form of the word* **peach** *is* **peaches**. *Say* **peaches**. (peaches) *What sound do the letters* **es** *have at the end of* **peaches**? (/ĭz/) Repeat this process for the remaining examples. Then read the directions and call students' attention to number 1. Say: *Read the word below the picture.* (box) *Does the picture show one box or more than one box?* (more than one box) *What do you add to* **box** *to make it plural?* (es) *Write the word* **boxes** *on the line.* Repeat this process for the remaining words.

Dictation   Direct students' attention to the bottom of the page and say:

Listen to each word I say. Then write the word you hear.   1. mixes   2. inches   3. wishes

DAY 3

Writing Words with Plural Endings

Read aloud the focus statement. Then point to the example and say: *The first word is* **fly**. *It ends with the consonant* **l** *and a* **y**. *Say* **fly**. (fly) *To make the word* **fly** *plural, the* **y** *is changed to* **ies**. *What is the new word?* (flies) *What sound do you hear at the end?* (/z/) Then read the directions and call students' attention to number 1. Say: *Read the word below the picture.* (spy) *Does the picture show one spy or more than one spy?* (more than one spy) *What word do you write to make* **spy** *plural?* (spies) *Write the word* **spies** *on the line.* Repeat this process for the remaining words.

Dictation   Direct students' attention to the bottom of the page and say:

Listen to each pair of words I say. Then write the words you hear.   1. sky   skies   2. story   stories

DAY 4

Writing Words with Plural Endings

Read aloud the focus statement. Then point to the example and say: *This word is* **calf**. *It ends in the letter* **f**. *Say* **calf**. (calf) *To make the word* **calf** *plural, the* **f** *is changed to* **ves**. *The plural of* **calf** *is* **calves**. *The word* **calves** *means more than one* **calf**. *You can hear the* /v/ *sound in* **calves**. *Say* **calves**. (calves) Then read the directions and call students' attention to number 1. Say: *Read the word below the picture.* (elf) *What is the plural form of elf?* (elves) *Write the plural form on the line.* Repeat this process for the remaining words.

Dictation   Direct students' attention to the bottom of the page and say:

Listen to each pair of words I say. Then write the words you hear.   1. self   selves   2. wife   wives

DAY 5

Reading Plural Words

Read the directions and call students' attention to the word box. Have students read the words aloud. Then say: *Let's read number 1 together: The* _____ *wore dark glasses. Which word from the word box makes the most sense in this sentence?* (spies) *Write* **spies** *on the line.* Have students complete the remaining sentences independently. After they finish, guide students in reading the completed sentences.

Dictation   Direct students' attention to the bottom of the page and say:

Listen to this sentence: **The elves made dresses for the babies.** *Write the words on the line.*

Name _____

Read It

Focus When a word has an **s** added to the end, it shows more than one. The **s** makes the word plural. The **s** can have the /s/ or /z/ sound.

 | bear + **s** = bears |

Look at the picture. Read the words.
Then fill in the circle next to the correct word.

1.

○ nut   ○ nuts

2.

○ hawk   ○ hawks

3.

○ cake   ○ cakes

4.

○ chain   ○ chains

5.

○ mask   ○ masks

6.

○ comb   ○ combs

7.

○ chair   ○ chairs

8.

○ skunk   ○ skunks

9.
○ clown   ○ clowns

Dictation •

1. _____   2. _____   3. _____   4. _____

Write It

Focus
Some words have **es** added to the end to make them plural.
An **es** is added to words that end in **ch**, **sh**, **ss**, or **x**.

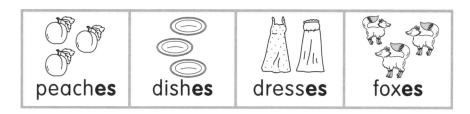

| peach**es** | dish**es** | dress**es** | fox**es** |

Look at the picture. Read the word.
Then write the **plural** form of the word on the line.

1.

box

_____

2.

dish

_____

3.

couch

_____

4.

glass

_____

5.

brush

_____

6.

lunch

_____

Dictation •

1. _____   2. _____   3. _____

Write It

Focus When a word ends in a **consonant** and a **y**, the **y** is changed to **ies** to make the word plural. The letter **s** has the /z/ sound.

| fly | fly + **ies** = flies | flies |

Make the word plural. Change the **y** to **ies**.
Then read the word you wrote.

1.

spy

_____

2.

pony

_____

3.

berry

_____

4.

candy

_____

5.

cherry

_____

6.

penny

_____

7.

puppy

_____

8.

lady

_____

9.

fry

_____

Dictation •

1. _____ _____   2. _____ _____

Write It

Focus When a word ends in **f**, the **f** is changed to **ves** to make the word plural.

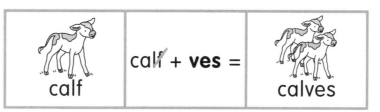

| calf | calf + **ves** = | calves |

Make the word plural. Change the **f** to **v** and add **es**.
Then read the word you wrote.

1.

elf

_____

2.

half

_____

3.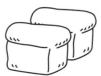

loaf

_____

4.

scarf

_____

5.

wolf

_____

6.

leaf

_____

7.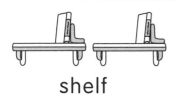

shelf

_____

8.

thief

_____

9.

knife

_____

Dictation •

1. _____ _____   2. _____ _____

Read It

Word Box

cookies	foxes	dishes	flies
peaches	scarves	spies	kisses

Write the word that completes the sentence.
Then read the sentence out loud.

1. The _____ wore dark glasses.

2. Our new set of cups and _____ came in big boxes.

3. Wolves and _____ have bushy tails.

4. Big black _____ buzzed around the ponies.

5. Cherries, plums, and _____ have pits.

6. Mom gave the babies many hugs and _____.

7. I will bake two batches of yummy _____.

8. The ladies have new red dresses and _____.

Dictation

_____

DAY 1 — Listening for Irregular Plural Nouns

Read aloud the focus statement. If necessary, review the terms **singular** and **plural**. Then point to the first example and say: *Read these words with me: **foot, feet**. How did the vowels change to show more than one?* (the digraph oo changed to ee) *Which letters did <u>not</u> change?* (f, t) Point to the second example and say: *Read these words with me: **child, children**. Which word shows more than one?* (children) *How is the plural word different?* (The vowel sound changed from /ī/ to /ĭ/ and ren was added at the end.) Then read the directions and call students' attention to number 1. Say: *Read the word with me.* (man) *The plural form of **man** is **men**. Say **men**.* (men) *Find the word **men**. Draw a line from the word **man** to the word **men**. How did the plural word change?* (The a changed to an e.) Repeat this process for the remaining words.

Dictation   Direct students' attention to the bottom of the page and say:

Listen to each word I say. Then write the plural form.   1. man   2. tooth   3. mouse

DAY 2 — Writing Irregular Plural Nouns

Read the directions and call students' attention to the word box. Have them read the words aloud. Then say: *Now look at the first word. What does it say?* (mouse) *Is **mouse** singular or plural?* (singular) *Write the word **mouse** in the column labeled **one**.* When students have finished writing, say: *Now find the plural form of **mouse** in the word box and write it in the column labeled **more than one**.* Repeat this process for the remaining words.

Dictation   Direct students' attention to the bottom of the page and say:

*Listen to this sentence: **Do mice have teeth?** Write the words on the line.*

DAY 3 — Writing Irregular Plural Nouns

Read aloud the focus statement. Point to the first example and say: *The plural form of the word **deer** is the same as its singular form. We say **deer** when we are talking about one deer or more than one deer. Now look at the pictures of the jeans. We say **jeans** when we talk about one pair of jeans or more than one pair of jeans.* Then read the directions and call students' attention to number 1. Say: *The first picture shows a sheep. Let's read the phrase together: **one sheep**. Does the next picture show one sheep or more than one sheep?* (more than one sheep.) *More than one sheep is also called **sheep**. Let's read the phrase together: **a flock of _____**. What is the plural of **sheep**?* (sheep) *Write the word **sheep** on the line.* Repeat this process for the remaining phrases.

Dictation   Direct students' attention to the bottom of the page and say:

*Listen and follow my directions: 1. Write the plural form of **deer**. 2. Write the singular form of **jeans**. 3. Write the singular form of **sheep**. 4. Write the plural form of **shorts**.*

DAY 4 — Writing Irregular Plural Nouns

Read the directions and call students' attention to number 1. Say: *Let's read the phrase next to the first picture: **one mouse**. Now let's read the incomplete phrase next to the second picture: **many _____**. What is the plural form of **mouse**?* (mice) *How do you spell **mice**?* (m-i-c-e) *Write the word **mice** on the line.* After students finish writing, say: *Now let's read the completed phrase together: **many mice**.* Have students complete the activity independently. After they finish, have students read their answers.

Dictation   Direct students' attention to the bottom of the page and say:

*Listen to this sentence: **The children saw some geese.** Write the words on the line.*

DAY 5 — Reading Irregular Plural Nouns

Read the directions and call students' attention to number 1. Say: *Let's read the incomplete sentence together: **Some of the _____ wore sunglasses.** The word **some** is a clue that tells us that more than one person wore sunglasses. Now let's read the two word choices: **man, men**. Which word means more than one?* (men) *Write the word **men** on the line.* After students finish writing, say: *Now let's read the sentence together: **Some of the men wore sunglasses.*** Repeat this process for the remaining sentences. Encourage students to suggest the clues that indicate a plural word is needed.

Word Clues: 1. some, 2. geese, 3. three, 4. all, 5. socks, 6. many

Dictation   Direct students' attention to the bottom of the page and say:

*Listen to this sentence: **The people saw many sheep on the hill.** Write the words on the line.*

Listen for It

Focus Some plural forms of words are very different from their singular forms. The vowels might change or the whole word might change.

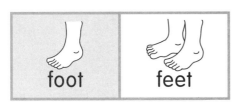

Read the word. Then draw a line to its plural form.

1. man   • people

2. woman   • teeth

3. goose   • mice

4. tooth   • women

5. mouse   • men

6. person   • geese

Dictation ••

1. man _____   2. tooth _____   3. mouse _____

Write It

Word Box

mouse	teeth	feet	foot
geese	child	woman	children
tooth	women	mice	goose

Read each word in the box above. If the word is singular, write it under **one**.
If the word is plural, write it under **more than one**.

singular **one**	plural **more than one**
_____	_____
_____	_____
_____	_____
_____	_____
_____	_____
_____	_____

Dictation •

_____

Write It

Focus Some words have the same singular and plural forms. The spellings do not change.

 deer | deer   jeans | jeans

The words in bold type have the same singular and plural forms.
Write the plural form of the word on the line.

1.  one **sheep**   a flock of _____

2.  black **pants**   two pairs of _____

3. a **moose**   three _____

4. one **deer**   many _____

5. my **glasses**   some cute _____

6. a pair of **shorts**   two pairs of _____

Dictation

1. _____   2. _____   3. _____   4. _____

Write It

Read the first pair of words in each row. Then write the plural form of the word that appears in bold type.

1. one **mouse**   many _____

2. my **shorts**   these _____

3. a **man**   a group of _____

4. your **foot**   your _____

5. a **deer**   a herd of _____

6. one **tooth**   many _____

7. one **child**   four _____

Dictation •

_____

Read It

Write the word that completes the sentence.
Then read the sentence out loud.

1. Some of the _____ wore sunglasses.
   man   men

2. Geese do not have _____.
   tooth   teeth

3. Five deer ran past three _____.
   moose   meese

4. All the _____ fled when they saw the mice.
   person   people

5. These socks are too big for my _____.
   foot   feet

6. Many _____ tried on jeans at the store.
   women   woman

Dictation •••

_____

Inflectional Verb Endings
-ed, -ing, -s, -es

DAY 1

Writing Words with Inflectional Endings

Read aloud the focus statement. Then point to the first column of the example chart and say: *Read the sentence with me: I help.* Ask: *What is the action word, or the verb?* (help) *Read aloud the sentence in the second column with me: I helped.* Ask: *What letters were added to the word **help**?* (ed) *What sound do you hear at the end of **helped**?* (/t/) Repeat this process for **helping**. Explain that the letters **ing** together have the /ĭng/ sound. Then read the directions and call students' attention to number 1. Say: *Let's read the first word together: **ask**. Write **ask** with the **ed** ending. Then write **ask** with the **ing** ending.* After students finish writing, say: *Read the first word you wrote.* (asked) *What sound do you hear at the end of **asked**?* (/t/) *Now read the other word you wrote.* (asking) Repeat this process for the remaining rows. For **ended**, **visited**, and **painted**, point out that when **ed** is added to a base word ending with **d** or **t**, the **ed** is pronounced /ĕd/.

Dictation Direct students' attention to the bottom of the page and say:

Listen to each word I say. Then write the word you hear. 1. *sending* 2. *bumped* 3. *wished*

DAY 2

Writing Words with Inflectional Endings

Read aloud the focus statement. Then point to the first column of the example chart and say: *Read the sentence with me: I hike.* Ask: *What is the action word?* (hike) *Does **hike** end with a consonant and a silent e?* (yes) *Read aloud the second example sentence with me: I hiked. The final e was dropped from **hike**, and **ed** was added to spell **hiked**. The i in **hiked** has a long sound.* Repeat this process for **hiking**. Then read the directions and guide students through the activity. Point out the pronunciation differences for the words that end with **ed** (/t/, /d/, and /ĕd/).

Dictation Direct students' attention to the bottom of the page and say:

Listen to each word I say. Then write the word you hear. 1. *saved* 2. *taping* 3. *voted*

DAY 3

Writing Words with Inflectional Endings

Read aloud the focus statement. Then point to the first column of the example chart and say: *Read the sentence with me: I jog. Now read aloud the sentence in the second column with me: I jogged.* Ask: *What letters were added to the word **jog**?* (g and ed) *We doubled the letter **g** and added the letters **ed** to spell **jogged**.* Repeat this process for **jogging**. Then read the directions and guide students through the activity. Point out the pronunciation differences for the words that end with **ed** (/t/, /d/, and /ĕd/). After students finish writing all the words, have them read each row of words aloud.

Dictation Direct students' attention to the bottom of the page and say:

Listen to each word I say. Then write the word you hear. 1. *hopping* 2. *stopped* 3. *slipped*

DAY 4

Writing Words with Inflectional Endings

Read aloud the focus statement. Then point to each example box and read the words aloud. Point out the /ĭz/ sound at the end of **mixes**. Then read the directions and guide students through the activity. After they finish, have them read aloud each word they wrote.

Dictation Direct students' attention to the bottom of the page and say:

Listen to each word I say. Then write the word you hear. 1. *wishes* 2. *mixes* 3. *drips*

DAY 5

Reading Words with Inflectional Endings

Read the directions and call students' attention to number 1. Say: *Let's read the incomplete sentence together: Ray _____ as he _____ the dishes. Now let's read the word choices: **washed, hummed, jumped**. Which word belongs on the first line?* (hummed) *Write **hummed** on the line. Which word belongs on the second line?* (washed) *Write the word **washed** to complete the sentence.* After students finish writing, say: *Let's read the sentence together: **Ray hummed as he washed the dishes**.* Repeat this process for the remaining sentences.

Dictation Direct students' attention to the bottom of the page and say:

*Listen to this sentence: **I am hoping that we can go skating**. Write the words on the line.*

Write It

Focus Most verbs are action words. When a verb ends in **ed**, it means the action has already happened. When a verb ends with **ing**, it means the action is or was in the process of happening.

action	+ **ed**	+ **ing**
I help.	I help**ed**.	I am help**ing**. I was help**ing**.

Read the action word. Write it with each ending.
Then read the new words you wrote. Listen for the sound **ed** has in each word.

action (base word)	+ **ed**	+ **ing**
1. ask	_____	_____
2. turn	_____	_____
3. pass	_____	_____
4. grill	_____	_____
5. end	_____	_____
6. visit	_____	_____
7. paint	_____	_____

Dictation •••

1. _____ 2. _____ 3. _____

Write It

Focus When a verb ends with a **silent e**, you drop the e before adding **ed** or **ing**. The first vowel in the verb has a long sound.

action	+ ed	+ ing
I hike.	I hik**ed**.	I am hik**ing**. I was hik**ing**.

Read the action word. Then write the word and follow the rule to add **ed**.
Write the word again and follow the rule to add **ing**.

action (base word)	+ ed	+ ing
1. joke	_____	_____
2. wave	_____	_____
3. hope	_____	_____
4. wipe	_____	_____
5. fade	_____	_____
6. chase	_____	_____
7. skate	_____	_____

Dictation •

1. _____   2. _____   3. _____

Write It

Focus When a verb ends with one short vowel and one consonant, the final consonant is doubled before **ing** or **ed** is added. The first vowel has a short sound.

action	+ ed	+ ing
I jog.	I jogg**ed**.	I am jogg**ing**. I was jogg**ing**.

Read the action word. Then write the word and follow the rule to add **ed**.
Write the word again and follow the rule to add **ing**.

action (base word)	+ ed	+ ing
1. rip	_____	_____
2. flip	_____	_____
3. brag	_____	_____
4. grin	_____	_____
5. drop	_____	_____
6. plan	_____	_____
7. skid	_____	_____

Dictation •

1. _____ 2. _____ 3. _____

Write It

Focus Sometimes a verb has an **s** or an **es** added to it. You add an **s** when a verb ends in a **consonant** or a **silent e**. You add **es** when a verb ends in **ch**, **sh**, **ss**, or **x**. The **es** sounds like /ĭz/.

gra**b** gra**bs**	rea**ch** reach**es**	pu**sh** push**es**	mi**ss** miss**es**	mi**x** mix**es**

Read the word. Then write the word and follow the rule to add **s or es**.
Read the new word you wrote.

1.
toss

_____

2.
fix

_____

3.
wash

_____

4.
jump

_____

5.
itch

_____

6.
pass

_____

7.
rush

_____

8.
drop

_____

9.
watch

_____

Dictation ....

1. _____   2. _____   3. _____

Read It

Write the words that complete the sentence.
Then read the sentence out loud.

1. washed   hummed   jumped

   Ray _____ as he _____ the dishes.

2. tossed   dropped   slipped

   I _____ the ball to Jacob, but he _____ it.

3. itching   itches   wishes

   Chad _____ his bug bite would stop _____.

4. flipped   ripped   hummed

   Ava _____ her jeans when she _____ over.

5. joining   planning   wishing

   Rosa is _____ on _____ us today.

Dictation

_____

DAY 1 — Reading Contractions

Read aloud the focus statement. Then point to the example and say: *The words **that is** can be written as the contraction **that's**. What letter was dropped from **that's**?* (the i in is) *What replaced the letter **i**?* (an apostrophe) Repeat this process for **you're**. Then read the directions and call students' attention to number 1. Say: *Let's read the contraction together: **it's**. Which two words form the contraction **it's**?* (it is) *Write the words **it is** on the line.* Repeat this process for the remaining contractions.

Dictation   Direct students' attention to the bottom of the page and say:

Listen to each sentence. Then write the words on the line.   1. He's tall.   2. It's hot!   3. Who's that?

DAY 2 — Reading Contractions

Read aloud the focus statement. Then point to the example and say: *The words **I had** can be written as the contraction **I'd**. What letters were dropped from **I'd**?* (ha in had) *What replaced **ha**?* (an apostrophe) Repeat this process for **we'll**. Then read the directions and call students' attention to number 1. Say: *Let's read the contraction together: **I'll**. Which two words form the contraction **I'll**?* (I will) *Write the words **I will** on the line.* Repeat this process for the remaining contractions.

Dictation   Direct students' attention to the bottom of the page and say:

Listen to each sentence. Then write the words on the line.   1. I'd better ask.   2. We'll go soon.

DAY 3 — Reading Contractions

Read aloud the focus statement. Then point to the example and say: *The words **is not** can be written as the contraction **isn't**. What letters were dropped from **isn't**?* (o in not) *What replaced the **o**?* (an apostrophe) Read the directions and call students' attention to number 1. Say: *Let's read the contraction together: **don't**. Which two words form the contraction **don't**?* (do not) *Write the words **do not** on the line.* Repeat this process for the remaining contractions.

Dictation   Direct students' attention to the bottom of the page and say:

Listen to each sentence. Then write the words on the line.   1. She can't meet us.   2. He isn't here.

DAY 4 — Reading Contractions

Read the directions and call students' attention to number 1. Say: *Read the word pair.* (does not) *What is the contraction for **does not**?* (doesn't) *Draw a line from **does not** to the contraction **doesn't**.* Have students complete the activity independently. After they finish, review the answers as a group.

Dictation   Direct students' attention to the bottom of the page and say:

Listen to each word pair I say. Write the contraction for the word pair on the line.
1. was not   2. I am   3. we are

DAY 5 — Writing Contractions

Read the directions and call students' attention to number 1. Say: *Let's read the incomplete sentence together: **Emma _____ know that it's raining**. Now read the word pair below the line: **does not**. Write the contraction for **does not** on the line.* After students finish writing, say: *Now let's read the sentence together: **Emma doesn't know that it's raining**.* Repeat this process for the remaining sentences.

Dictation   Direct students' attention to the bottom of the page and say:

Listen to each sentence. Then write the words on the line.   1. Don't cry.   2. Dad hasn't called me.

Read It

Focus A **contraction** is a short way of writing two words. An **apostrophe** shows that one or more letters has been left out. Many contractions are formed using the verbs **is** or **are**.

that ~~is~~ = that's	you ~~are~~ = you're

Read the contraction. Then write the two words that form the contraction.

1. it's _____

2. he's _____

3. they're _____

4. here's _____

5. who's _____

6. how's _____

7. we're _____

8. she's _____

9. what's _____

10. where's _____

Dictation ∙∙

1. _____ 2. _____ 3. _____

Read It

Focus Many contractions are formed using the verbs **had** or **will**.

| I had = I'd | we will = we'll |

Read the contraction. Then write the two words that form the contraction.

1. I'll _____

2. you'd _____

3. they'll _____

4. she'll _____

5. that'll _____

6. you'll _____

7. she'd _____

8. we'd _____

9. he'll _____

10. he'd _____

Dictation ⋯⋯⋯⋯⋯⋯⋯⋯⋯⋯⋯⋯⋯⋯⋯⋯⋯⋯⋯

1. _____ 2. _____

Read It

Focus   Many contractions are formed using the adverb **not**.

is not = isn't

Read the contraction. Then write the two words that form the contraction.

1. don't _____

2. can't _____

3. hadn't _____

4. couldn't _____

5. wasn't _____

6. hasn't _____

7. aren't _____

8. weren't _____

Dictation •

1. _____   2. _____

Skill: Reading contractions   **181**

Read It

Read each pair of words. Draw a line from the words to the correct contraction.
Then read the contraction out loud.

1. does not   • we'll

2. who is   • what's

3. you are   • they're

4. you will   • who's

5. we will   • you'll

6. what is   • you're

7. should not   • doesn't

8. they are   • shouldn't

Dictation

1. was not _____   2. I am _____   3. we are _____

Write It

Write the contraction for each pair of words.
Then read the sentence out loud.

1. Emma _____ know that it's raining.

does not

2. We'll ask Mom if _____ bake cookies.

she will

3. _____ the reason he's late for the game?

what is

4. I'm sure that this _____ the right street.

is not

5. I've washed the car, but _____ done nothing.

you have

6. She's saying that we _____ go with you.

can not

Dictation ....

1. _____   2. _____

DAY 1 **Writing Words with Prefixes**

Read aloud the focus statement. Then point to the prefix **un** and say: *The prefix* **un** *means "not" or "the opposite of." Say* **un**. (un) Repeat this process for **re**. Then point to the first example in the gray box as you say: *When* **un** *is added to* **kind**, *what new word is formed?* (unkind) Repeat this process for the second example box. Then read the directions and call students' attention to number 1. Say: *Let's read the base word together:* **pack**. *When you add* **un** *to* **pack**, *what new word is formed?* (unpack) *What does* **unpack** *mean?* (to do the opposite of pack) *Write* **unpack** *on the line.* After students finish writing, ask: *When you add* **re** *to* **pack**, *what new word is formed?* (repack) *What does* **repack** *mean?* (to pack something again) *Write* **repack** *on the next line.* Repeat this process for the remaining words.

Dictation Direct students' attention to the bottom of the page and say:
Listen to each word I say. Then write the word you hear.   1. undo   2. refill   3. repeat

---

DAY 2 **Writing Words with Prefixes**

Read aloud the focus statement. Then point to the prefix **dis** and say: *The prefix* **dis** *means "not." For example,* **disobey** *means "to not obey." The prefix* **re** *means "again." For example,* **rewash** *means to "wash again." The prefix* **un** *means "not." For example,* **unkind** *means "to not be kind."* Then read the directions and call students' attention to number 1. Say: *Let's read the first word together:* **rerun**. *What is the prefix in the word* **rerun**? (re) *Underline the prefix* **re**. *What does* **rerun** *mean?* (to run again) *Write* **run** *on the line.* Have students write the remaining meanings independently. After students finish, review the answers as a group.

Dictation Direct students' attention to the bottom of the page and say:
Listen to each word I say. Then write the word you hear.   1. repack   2. unzip   3. discover

---

DAY 3 **Writing Words with Prefixes**

Read the directions and call students' attention to number 1. Say: *Let's read the definition together:* **not even**. *Now let's try each prefix from the gray boxes with* **even** *to see which one sounds correct:* **diseven, reeven, uneven**. *Which word is correct?* (uneven) *Write the prefix* **un** *next to the word* **even**. *Then write the word* **uneven** *on the next line to the right.* Repeat this process for the remaining definitions.

Dictation Direct students' attention to the bottom of the page and say:
Listen to this sentence: **I will unlock the door.** *Write the words on the line.*

DAY 4 **Writing Words with Prefixes**

Read the directions and call students' attention to number 1. Say: *Let's read the incomplete sentence together:* **Jan will _____ fill the car with gas.** *Now point to the prefixes in the box at the top of the page. Which prefix belongs with the word* **fill**—**disfill, refill,** *or* **unfill**? (refill) *Write* **re** *on the line next to* **fill**. *Now let's read the sentence together:* **Jan will refill the car with gas.** Have students complete the remaining sentences independently. After students finish, guide them in reading the completed sentences.

Dictation Direct students' attention to the bottom of the page and say:
Listen to this sentence: **Will you reseal the bag?** *Write the words on the line.*

DAY 5 **Reading Words with Prefixes**

Read the directions and call students' attention to number 1. Say: *Let's read the incomplete sentence together:* **I helped Dad _____ the bags from the car.** *Now point to the words below the line. Let's read them together:* **unload, unseal**. *Which word completes the sentence?* (unload) *Write* **unload** *on the line.* After students finish writing, say: *Now let's read the sentence together:* **I helped Dad unload the bags from the car.** Have students complete the remaining sentences independently. After students finish, guide them in reading the completed sentences.

Dictation Direct students' attention to the bottom of the page and say:
Listen to this sentence: **I want to reread the book.** *Write the words on the line.*

Write It

Focus — A prefix is a word part added to the **beginning** of a word. Each prefix has a meaning. Knowing what a prefix means helps you know what a word means.

un = not, or the opposite of
un + kind = **un**kind

re = again
re + play = **re**play

Add each prefix to the beginning of the base word.
Write the two new words on the lines. Then read the words you wrote.

base word	un	re
1. pack	_____	_____
2. tie	_____	_____
3. done	_____	_____
4. cover	_____	_____
5. paid	_____	_____
6. wrap	_____	_____
7. seal	_____	_____
8. load	_____	_____

Dictation ....

1. _____   2. _____   3. _____

Name _____

Write It

Focus   Each prefix has a meaning. Knowing what a prefix means helps you know what a word means.

| **dis** = not | **re** = again | **un** = not, or the opposite of |

Read the word in bold type. Underline the prefix.
Then complete the meaning of the word.

1. **rerun**	2. **uneven**	3. **dislike**
to _____ again	not _____	to not _____
4. **disallow**	5. **refill**	6. **unkind**
to not _____	to _____ again	not _____
7. **unsure**	8. **rewrite**	9. **disagree**
not _____	to _____ again	to not _____

Dictation ....

1. _____   2. _____   3. _____

Write It

| **dis** = not | **re** = again | **un** = not, or the opposite of |

Read the definition. Write the correct prefix in front of the base word.
Then write the new word.

1. not even   _____even   _____

2. to read again   _____read   _____

3. to paint again   _____paint   _____

4. not happy   _____happy   _____

5. to not agree   _____agree   _____

6. not sure   _____sure   _____

7. to not trust   _____trust   _____

8. to count again   _____count   _____

Dictation •

_____

Write It

Prefix Box

dis	re	un

One word in each sentence is missing a prefix.
Write the correct prefix to complete the word. Then read the sentence.

1. Jan will _____fill the car with gas.

2. I'm _____happy that my dog ate my shoe.

3. Daniel and Megan _____like bananas.

4. We will _____pack our bags after our trip.

5. I'll _____write my messy homework.

6. Mom and I _____agree over my bedtime.

7. My dad will _____paint my bedroom.

Dictation •

_____

Read It

Write the word that completes the sentence.
Then read the sentence out loud.

1. I helped Dad _____ the bags from the car.
   unload   unseal

2. I _____ eating cold pizza.
   distrust   dislike

3. Let's _____ the leftover pizza for lunch.
   remove   reheat

4. Chen will _____ the story a second time.
   retell   rewash

5. That water is _____ so don't drink it.
   unload   unclean

6. I _____ with your answer.
   dislike   disagree

Dictation •

_____

DAY 1

Writing Words with Suffixes

Read aloud the focus statement. Then point to the suffix **ful** and say: *The suffix **ful** means "full of." Say **full**.* (full) Repeat the process for **less**. Then point to the first example in the gray box as you ask: *When **ful** is added to the end of **color**, what new word is formed?* (colorful) Repeat this process for the second example box. Then read the directions and call students' attention to number 1. Say: *Let's read the base word together: **help**. When you add **ful** to the end of **help**, what new word is formed?* (helpful) *What does **helpful** mean?* (full of help) *Write **helpful** on the line.* After students finish writing, ask: *When you add **less** to the end of **help**, what new word is formed?* (helpless) *What does **helpless** mean?* (without help) *Write **helpless** on the next line to the right.* Repeat this process for the remaining words.

Dictation Direct students' attention to the bottom of the page and say:

Listen to each word I say. Then write the word you hear.   1. *useful*   2. *harmless*   3. *playful*

DAY 2

Writing Words with Suffixes

Read the directions and call students' attention to number 1. Say: *Let's read the definition together: **without care**. Which suffix means **without**?* (less) *Write the suffix **less** on the line next to **care**. What's the new word?* (careless) *Write the word **careless** on the next line.* Repeat this process for the remaining definitions.

Dictation Direct students' attention to the bottom of the page and say:

*Listen to this sentence: **My mom is cheerful.** Write the words on the line.*

DAY 3

Writing Words with Suffixes

Read aloud the focus statement. Then point to the suffix **er** and say: *The suffix **er** means "someone who." Say **er**.* (er) Repeat this process for **ly**. Then point to the first example in the gray box as you ask: *When **er** is added to the end of **paint**, what new word is formed?* (painter) Repeat this process for the second example box. Then read the directions and call students' attention to the first column. Say: *Point to number 1. Let's read the base word together: **play**. When you add **er** to **play**, what new word is formed?* (player) *For example, **Who is the first player in the game?** Write **player** on the line.* Repeat this process for the remaining words and suffixes.

Dictation Direct students' attention to the bottom of the page and say:

*Listen to this sentence: **The waiter took my order.** Write the words on the line.*

DAY 4

Writing Words with Suffixes

Read the directions and call students' attention to number 1. Say: *Let's read the incomplete sentence together: **The farm_____ grows corn.** Now point to the suffixes in the box at the top of the page. Which suffix belongs with the word **farm**—**farmer**, **farmful**, **farmless**, or **farmly**?* (farmer) *Write **er** on the line next to **farm**. Now let's read the sentence together: **The farmer grows corn.*** Have students complete the remaining sentences independently. After they finish, guide students in reading the completed sentences.

Dictation Direct students' attention to the bottom of the page and say:

*Listen to this sentence: **A tiny puppy is helpless.** Write the words on the line.*

DAY 5

Reading Words with Suffixes

Read the directions and call students' attention to number 1. Say: *Let's read the incomplete sentence together: **The snow fell _____ from the black sky.** Now point to the words below the line. Let's read them together: **softly, sadly.** Which word completes the sentence?* (softly) *Write **softly** on the line.* After students finish writing, say: *Now let's read the sentence together: **The snow fell softly from the black sky.*** Have students complete the remaining sentences independently. After students finish, guide them in reading the completed sentences.

Dictation Direct students' attention to the bottom of the page and say:

*Listen to this sentence: **Lions seem fearless.** Write the words on the line.*

Write It

Focus A suffix is a word part added to the **end** of a word. Each suffix has a meaning. Knowing what a suffix means helps you know what a word means.

ful = full of
color + **ful** = color**ful**

less = without
fear + **less** = fear**less**

Add each suffix to the end of the base word.
Write the two new words on the lines. Then read the words you wrote.

base word	ful	less
1. help	_____	_____
2. use	_____	_____
3. power	_____	_____
4. care	_____	_____
5. harm	_____	_____
6. thank	_____	_____
7. pain	_____	_____
8. hope	_____	_____

Dictation ···

1. _____   2. _____   3. _____

Write It

Focus A suffix is a word part added to the **end** of a word. Each suffix has a meaning. Knowing what a suffix means helps you know what a word means.

ful = full of
fear**ful** = full of fear

less = without
fear**less** = without fear

Read the definition. Write the correct suffix after the base word. Then write the new word.

1. without care   care_____   _____

2. full of power   power_____   _____

3. full of cheer   cheer_____   _____

4. without fear   fear_____   _____

5. full of color   color_____   _____

6. without pain   pain_____   _____

7. full of peace   peace_____   _____

8. without use   use_____   _____

Dictation ···

_____

Write It

Focus Every suffix has a meaning. Knowing the meaning of a suffix can help you figure out the meaning of a word.

er = someone who
paint + **er** = painter

ly = in a certain way
quiet + **ly** = quietly

Read the base word.
Then write the word using the suffix **er** or **ly**. The first one is an example.

base word	er
1. play	player
2. sing	_____
3. work	_____
4. teach	_____
5. build	_____
6. surf	_____

base word	ly
1. quick	_____
2. loud	_____
3. soft	_____
4. sad	_____
5. kind	_____
6. near	_____

Dictation ••

_____

Write It

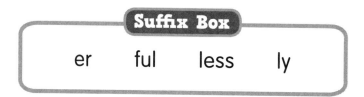

Suffix Box

er   ful   less   ly

One word in each sentence is missing a suffix.
Write the correct suffix to complete the word. Then read the sentence.

1. The farm_____ grows corn.

2. The cat jumped quiet_____ onto the bed.

3. A superhero is power_____.

4. The broken box was use_____.

5. Gramps was cheer_____ when he saw me.

6. The build_____ used bricks to make the house.

7. The nurse spoke kind_____ to me.

Dictation ....

_____

Read It

Write the word that completes the sentence.
Then read the sentence out loud.

1. The snow fell _____ from the black sky.
   softly   sadly

2. I was _____ and I spilled the paint.
   careful   careless

3. The _____ spun around the stage.
   digger   dancer

4. The lion roared _____ at the zebra.
   loudly   smoothly

5. A _____ wind knocked down the oak tree.
   powerless   powerful

6. I'm _____ that you drove me to school.
   thankless   thankful

Dictation ••

_____

Answer Key

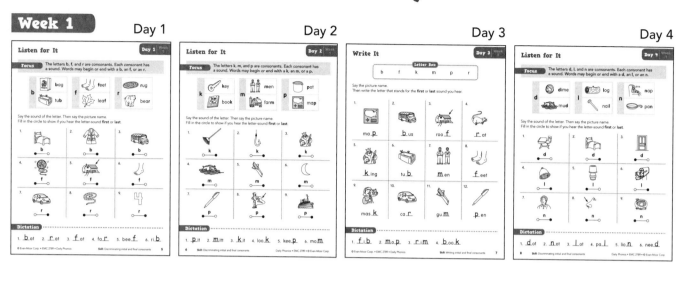

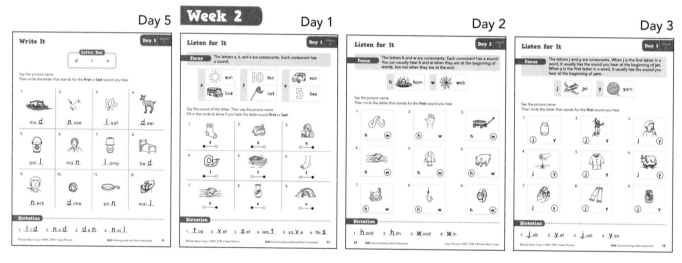

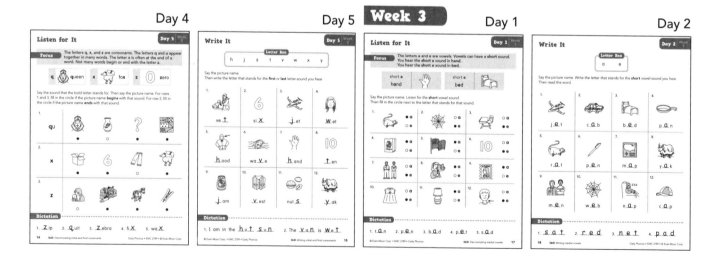

Day 3 Day 4 Day 5 Day 1

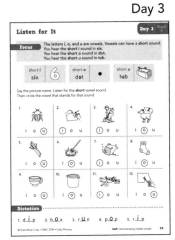   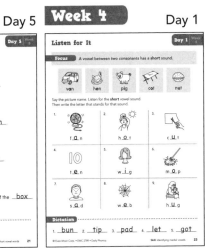

Day 2 Day 3 Day 4 Day 5

  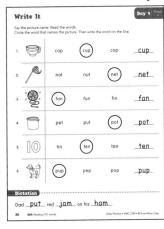 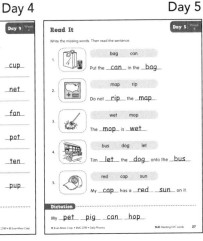

Week 5 Day 1 Day 2 Day 3 Day 4

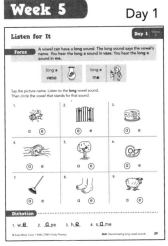 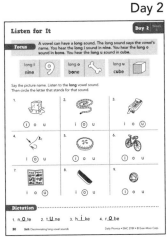 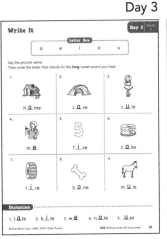 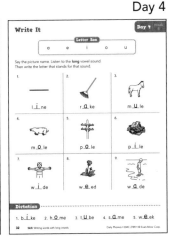

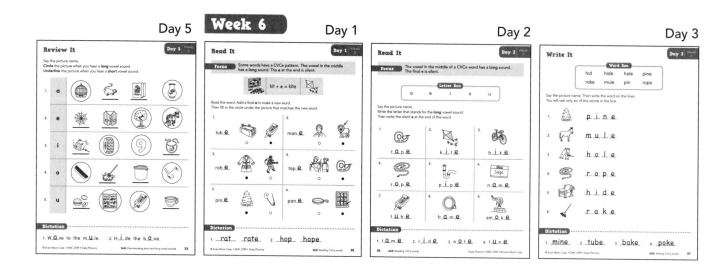

Day 5 · **Week 6** · **Day 1** · **Day 2** · **Day 3**

Day 5 — Review It

Say the picture name.
Circle the picture when you hear a **long** vowel sound.
Underline the picture when you hear a **short** vowel sound.

1. a
2. e
3. i
4. o
5. u

Dictation
1. W_a_ve to the m_u_le.   2. H_i_de the b_o_ne.

Day 1 — Read It

Focus Some words have a CVCe pattern. The vowel in the middle has a **long** sound. The **e** at the end is silent.

kit + e = kite

Read the word. Add a final **e** to make a new word.
Then fill in the circle under the picture that matches the new word.

1. tub_e_
2. man_e_
3. rob_e_
4. tap_e_
5. pin_e_
6. pan_e_

Dictation
1. _rat_ _rate_   2. _hop_ _hope_

Day 2 — Read It

Focus The vowel in the middle of a CVCe word has a **long** sound. The final **e** is silent.

Letter Box
a   e   i   o   u

Say the picture name.
Write the letter that stands for the long vowel sound.
Then write the silent **e** at the end of the word.

1. t_a_p_e_
2. k_i_t_e_
3. b_i_k_e_
4. r_o_p_e_
5. p_i_p_e_
6. n_a_m_e_
7. t_u_b_e_
8. fr_a_m_e_
9. sm_o_ke_

Dictation
1. t_a_m_e_   2. r_i_de   3. n_o_te   4. t_u_ne

Day 3 — Write It

Word Box
hid   hide   hole   pine
rake   mule   pin   rope

Say the picture name. Then write the word on the lines.
You will use only six of the words in the box.

1. p i n e
2. m u l e
3. h o l e
4. r o p e
5. h i d e
6. r a k e

Dictation
1. _mine_   2. _tube_   3. _bake_   4. _poke_

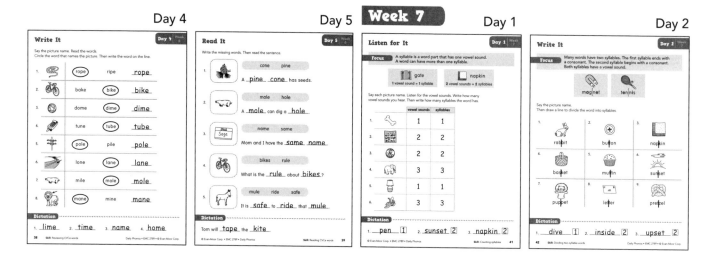

Day 4 · **Day 5** · **Week 7** · **Day 1** · **Day 2**

Day 4 — Write It

Say the picture name. Read the words.
Circle the word that names the picture. Then write the word on the line.

1. (rope) ripe   _rope_
2. bake (bike)   _bike_
3. dome (dime)   _dime_
4. tune (tube)   _tube_
5. (pole) pile   _pole_
6. lone (lane)   _lane_
7. mile (mole)   _mole_
8. (mane) mine   _mane_

Dictation
1. _lime_   2. _time_   3. _name_   4. _home_

Day 5 — Read It

Write the missing words. Then read the sentence.

1. cone   pine
   A _pine_ _cone_ has seeds.
2. mole   hole
   A _mole_ can dig a _hole_.
3. name   same
   Mom and I have the _same_ _name_.
4. bikes   rule
   What is the _rule_ about _bikes_?
5. mule   ride   safe
   It is _safe_ to _ride_ that _mule_.

Dictation
Tom will _tape_ the _kite_.

Day 1 — Listen for It

Focus A syllable is a word part that has one vowel sound. A word can have more than one syllable.

gate — 1 vowel sound = 1 syllable
napkin — 2 vowel sounds = 2 syllables

Say each picture name. Listen for the vowel sounds. Write how many vowel sounds you hear. Then write how many syllables the word has.

	vowel sounds	syllables
1.	1	1
2.	2	2
3.	2	2
4.	3	3
5.	1	1
6.	3	3

Dictation
1. _pen_ [1]   2. _sunset_ [2]   3. _napkin_ [2]

Day 2 — Write It

Focus Many words have two syllables. The first syllable ends with a consonant. The second syllable begins with a consonant. Both syllables have a vowel sound.

mag•net   ten•nis

Say the picture name.
Then draw a line to divide the word into syllables.

1. rab•bit   2. but•ton   3. nap•kin
4. bas•ket   5. muf•fin   6. sun•set
7. pup•pet   8. let•ter   9. pret•zel

Dictation
1. dive [1]   2. inside [2]   3. upset [2]

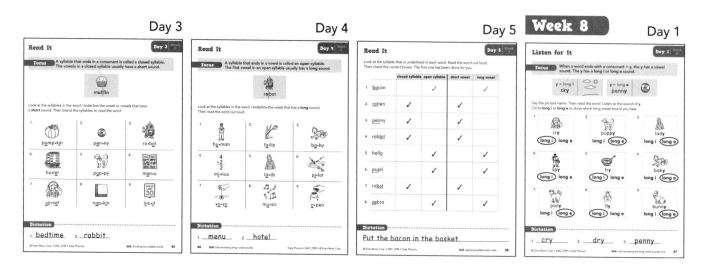

Day 3 · **Day 4** · **Day 5** · **Week 8** · **Day 1**

Day 3 — Read It

Focus A syllable that ends in a consonant is called a **closed syllable**. The vowels in a closed syllable usually have a **short** sound.

muf•fin

Look at the syllables in the word. Underline the vowel or vowels that have a **short** sound. Then blend the syllables to read the word.

1. pump•kin   2. pen•ny   3. ro•bot
4. ho•tel   5. pup•py   6. men•u
7. up•set   8. nap•kin   9. lim•it

Dictation
1. bedtime   2. _rabbit_

Day 4 — Read It

Focus A syllable that ends in a vowel is called an **open syllable**. The first vowel in an open syllable usually has a **long** sound.

ro•bot

Look at the syllables in the word. Underline the vowel that has a **long** sound. Then read the word out loud.

1. hu•man   2. tu•lip   3. ba•by
4. mi•nus   5. la•dy   6. pi•lot
7. yo•yo   8. mu•sic   9. o•pen

Dictation
1. _menu_   2. _hotel_

Day 5 — Read It

Look at the syllable that is underlined in each word. Read the word out loud. Then check the correct boxes. The first one has been done for you.

	closed syllable	open syllable	short vowel	long vowel
1. <u>ba</u>con		✓		✓
2. <u>rot</u>ten	✓		✓	
3. <u>pen</u>ny	✓		✓	
4. rab<u>bit</u>	✓		✓	
5. <u>hel</u>lo		✓		✓
6. <u>pu</u>pil		✓		✓
7. <u>ro</u>bot		✓		✓
8. <u>ze</u>bra		✓		✓

Dictation
Put the bacon in the basket.

Day 1 — Listen for It

Focus When a word ends with a consonant + y, the y has a vowel sound. The y has a **long i** or a **long e** sound.

y = long i   sky
y = long e   penny

Say the picture name. Then read the word out loud. Listen to the sound of y. Circle **long i** or **long e** to show which long vowel sound you hear.

1. cry — (long i) long e
2. puppy — long i (long e)
3. lady — long i (long e)
4. spy — (long i) long e
5. fry — (long i) long e
6. baby — long i (long e)
7. pony — long i (long e)
8. fly — (long i) long e
9. bunny — long i (long e)

Dictation
1. _cry_   2. _dry_   3. _penny_

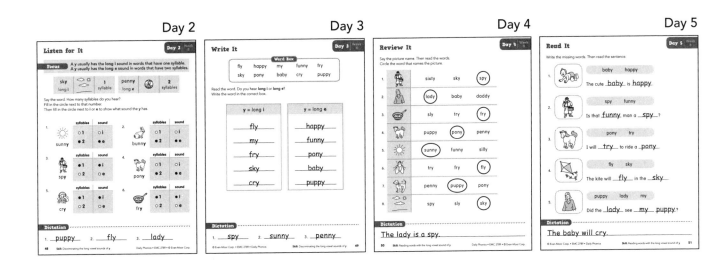

Day 2 · Day 3 · Day 4 · Day 5

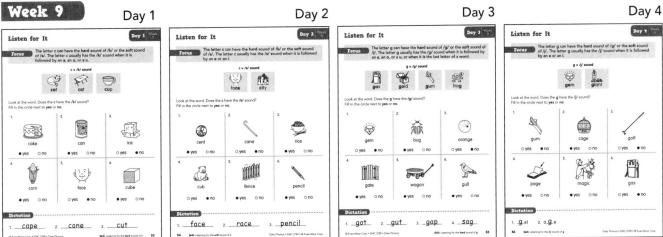

Week 9 · Day 1 · Day 2 · Day 3 · Day 4

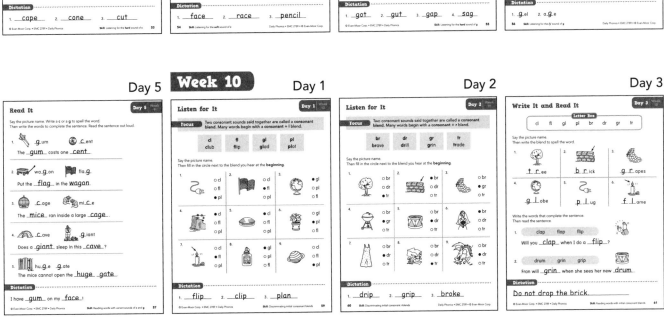

Day 5 · Week 10 · Day 1 · Day 2 · Day 3

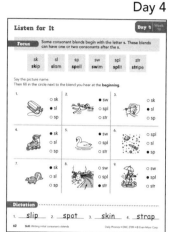

Listen for It — Day 4

Focus Some consonant blends begin with the letter s. These blends can have one or two consonants after the s.

sk	sl	sp	sw	spl	str
skip	slam	spell	swim	split	stripe

Say the picture name.
Then fill in the circle next to the blend you hear at the beginning.

Dictation
1. slip 2. spot 3. skin 4. strap

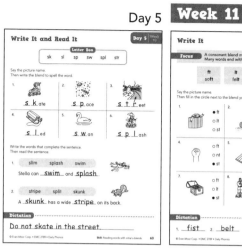

Write It and Read It — Day 5

Letter Box: sk sl sp sw spl str

Say the picture name.
Then write the blend to spell the word.
1. s k ate 2. s p ace 3. s t r eet
4. s l ed 5. s w an 6. s p l ash

Write the words that complete the sentence.
Then read the sentence.
1. slim splash swim
Stella can swim and splash.
2. stripe split skunk
A skunk has a wide stripe on its back.

Dictation
Do not skate in the street.

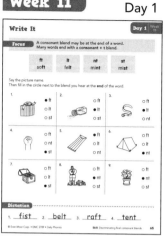

Write It — Day 1

Focus A consonant blend may be at the end of a word. Many words end with a consonant + t blend.

ft	lt	nt	st
soft	felt	mint	mist

Say the picture name.
Then fill in the circle next to the blend you hear at the end of the word.

Dictation
1. fist 2. belt 3. raft 4. tent

Write It — Day 2

Letter Box: ft lt nt st

Say the picture name. Write the blend to spell the word.
Then read the word.
1. ne s t 2. gi f t 3. te n t
4. be l t 5. ra f t 6. me l t
7. cru s t 8. ce n t 9. ca s t

Dictation
The vest felt soft.

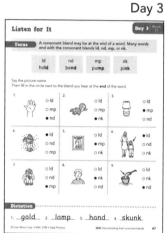

Listen for It — Day 3

Focus A consonant blend may be at the end of a word. Many words end with the consonant blends ld, nd, mp, or nk.

ld	nd	mp	nk
hold	bend	pump	pink

Say the picture name.
Then fill in the circle next to the blend you hear at the end of the word.

Dictation
1. gold 2. lamp 3. hand 4. skunk

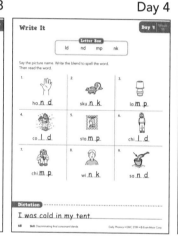

Write It — Day 4

Letter Box: ld nd mp nk

Say the picture name. Write the blend to spell the word.
Then read the word.
1. ha n d 2. sku n k 3. la m p
4. co l d 5. sta m p 6. chi l d
7. chi m p 8. wi n k 9. sa n d

Dictation
I was cold in my tent.

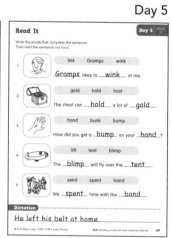

Read It — Day 5

Write the words that complete the sentence.
Then read the sentence out loud.
1. link Gramps wink
Gramps likes to wink at me.
2. gold hold host
The chest can hold a lot of gold.
3. hand bunk bump
How did you get a bump on your hand?
4. lift tent blimp
The blimp will fly over the tent.
5. send spent band
We spent time with the band.

Dictation
He left his belt at home.

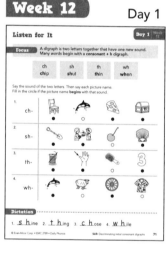

Listen for It — Day 1

Focus A digraph is two letters together that have one new sound. Many words begin with a consonant + h digraph.

ch	sh	th	wh
chip	shut	thin	when

Say the sound of the two letters. Then say each picture name.
Fill in the circle if the picture name begins with that sound.

1. ch-
2. sh-
3. th-
4. wh-

Dictation
1. s h ine 2. t h ing 3. c h ose 4. w h ile

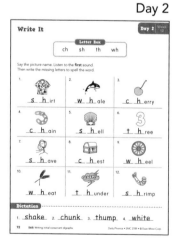

Write It — Day 2

Letter Box: ch sh th wh

Say the picture name. Listen to the first sound.
Then write the missing letters to spell the word.
1. s h irt 2. w h ale 3. c h erry
4. c h ain 5. s h ell 6. t h ree
7. s h ave 8. c h est 9. w h eel
10. w h eat 11. t h under 12. s h rimp

Dictation
1. shake 2. chunk 3. thump 4. white

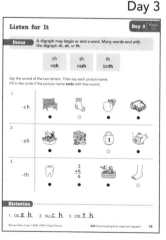

Listen for It — Day 3

Focus A digraph may begin or end a word. Many words end with the digraph ch, sh, or th.

ch	sh	th
rich	rash	both

Say the sound of the two letters. Then say each picture name.
Fill in the circle if the picture name ends with that sound.

1. -ch
2. -sh
3. -th

Dictation
1. ca s h 2. su c h 3. clo t h

Write It — Day 4

Letter Box: ch sh th

Say the picture name. Listen to the last sound.
Then write the missing letters to spell the word.
1. wa s h 2. pea c h 3. ba t h
4. ben c h 5. too t h 6. tra s h
7. sandwi c h 8. mo t h 9. fi s h
10. pa t h 11. bu s h 12. in c h

Dictation
1. math 2. fresh 3. bunch

Read It — Day 5

Write the words that complete the sentence.
Then read the sentence out loud.
1. both wash
We both have to wash the dog.
2. bush moth
A white moth landed on the bush.
3. ranch sheep
A flock of sheep live on that ranch.
4. chimp think
I think I see a chimp.
5. teeth whale
Does a whale have teeth?

Dictation
She will brush her teeth.

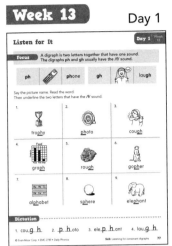
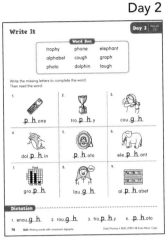

Week 13

Day 1

Listen for It

Focus A digraph is two letters together that have one sound. The digraphs ph and gh usually have the /f/ sound.

ph — phone   gh — laugh

Say the picture name. Read the word.
Then underline the two letters that have the /f/ sound.

1. trophy 2. photo 3. cough
4. graph 5. rough 6. gopher
7. alphabet 8. sphere 9. elephant

Dictation
1. cough 2. photo 3. elephant 4. laugh

Day 2

Write It

Word Box
trophy, phone, elephant, alphabet, cough, graph, photo, dolphin, laugh

Write the missing letters to complete the word.
Then read the word.

phone, trophy, cough, dolphin, photo, elephant, graph, laugh, alphabet

Dictation
1. enough 2. rough 3. trophy 4. photo

Day 3

Listen for It

Focus The letter pairs ck and ng are digraphs. The ck digraph has the /k/ sound. The ng digraph has the sound you hear at the end of ring. Many words end with these digraphs.

ck — clock   ng — ring

Say the picture name.
Then fill in the circle next to the digraph you hear at the **end** of the word.

Dictation
1. sock 2. wing 3. lung 4. brick

Day 4

Write It

Word Box
king, brick, lung, neck, clock, lock, ring, sing, truck

Say the picture name. Then write the word that names the picture.

1. king 2. lock 3. brick
4. lung 5. truck 6. ring
7. neck 8. sing 9. clock

Dictation
1. sick 2. trick 3. thing 4. sting

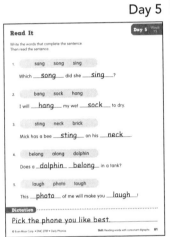
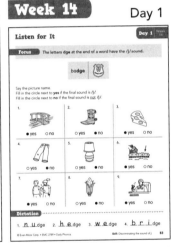
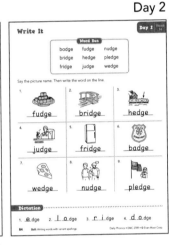

Day 5

Read It

Write the words that complete the sentence.
Then read the sentence.

1. sang song sing
   Which **song** did she **sing**?
2. bang sock hang
   I will **hang** my wet **sock** to dry.
3. sting neck brick
   Mick has a bee **sting** on his **neck**.
4. belong along dolphin
   Does a **dolphin belong** in a tank?
5. laugh photo tough
   This **photo** of me will make you **laugh**!

Dictation
Pick the phone you like best.

Week 14

Day 1

Listen for It

Focus The letters dge at the end of a word have the /j/ sound.

badge

Say the picture name.
Fill in the circle next to **yes** if the final sound is /j/.
Fill in the circle next to **no** if the final sound is **not** /j/.

Dictation
1. nudge 2. hedge 3. wedge 4. bridge

Day 2

Write It

Word Box
badge, fudge, nudge, bridge, hedge, pledge, fridge, judge, wedge

Say the picture name. Then write the word on the line.

1. fudge 2. bridge 3. hedge
4. judge 5. fridge 6. badge
7. wedge 8. nudge 9. pledge

Dictation
1. edge 2. lodge 3. ridge 4. dodge

Day 3

Listen for It

Focus The sound /ch/ can be spelled with the letters tch.

watch

Say the picture name.
Fill in the circle next to **yes** if the final sound is /ch/.
Fill in the circle next to **no** if the final sound is **not** /ch/.

Dictation
1. pitch 2. match 3. stretch

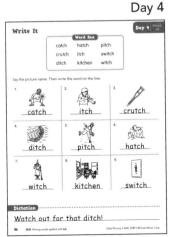

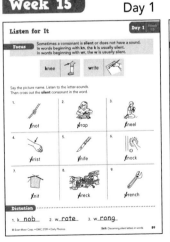

Day 4

Write It

Word Box
catch, hatch, pitch, crutch, itch, switch, ditch, kitchen, witch

Say the picture name. Then write the word on the line.

1. catch 2. itch 3. crutch
4. ditch 5. pitch 6. hatch
7. witch 8. kitchen 9. switch

Dictation
Watch out for that ditch!

Day 5

Read It

Write the word that completes the sentence.
Then read the sentence out loud.

1. Is the **fudge** in the fridge?
   nudge fudge
2. You **pitch** the ball, and I will catch it.
   patch pitch
3. A **judge** gave me a trophy at the end of the match.
   judge budge
4. My dog will **fetch** the stick by the hedge.
   sketch fetch
5. Do not stand at the **edge** of the ledge.
   badge edge
6. Does your badge **match** my badge?
   match hatch

Dictation
The latch will not budge!

Week 15

Day 1

Listen for It

Focus Sometimes a consonant is silent or does not have a sound. In words beginning with kn, the k is usually silent. In words beginning with wr, the w is usually silent.

knee   write

Say the picture name. Listen to the letter-sounds.
Then cross out the **silent** consonant in the word.

1. knot 2. wrap 3. kneel
4. wrist 5. knife 6. knock
7. knit 8. wreck 9. wrench

Dictation
1. knob 2. wrote 3. wrong

Day 2

Listen for It

Focus Sometimes the consonants b and h are silent.

comb   rhyme

Say the picture name. Listen to the letter-sounds.
Then cross out the **silent** consonant in the word.

1. lamb 2. ghost 3. thumb
4. hour 5. limb 6. crumb
7. climb 8. rhino 9. plumber

Dictation
1. limb 2. hour 3. thumb

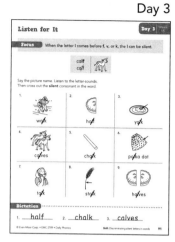

Listen for It — Day 3

Focus When the letter l comes before f, v, or k, it can be silent.

calf
calf

Say the picture name. Listen to the letter-sounds.
Then cross out the **silent** consonant in the word.

1. walk 2. half 3. yolk
4. calves 5. chalk 6. polka dot
7. talk 8. stalk 9. halves

Dictation
1. half   2. chalk   3. calves

© Evan-Moor Corp. • EMC 2789 • Daily Phonics   **Skill:** Discriminating silent letters in words   91

Write It — Day 4

Word Box
thumb rhino yolk
wrap knit comb
walk knee talk

Say the picture name. Then write the word on the line.

1. walk 2. yolk 3. wrap
4. comb 5. thumb 6. knee
7. knit 8. rhino 9. talk

Dictation
1. ghost   2. knit   3. wreck

92   Daily Phonics • EMC 2789 • © Evan-Moor Corp.

Read It — Day 5

Write the words that complete the sentence.
Then read the sentence out loud.

1. half calf knife
Use a __knife__ to cut the cake in __half__

2. climb walk crumb
You can __walk__ up the path and __climb__ the hill.

3. crumb lamb thumb
Pick up the __crumb__ with your __thumb__

4. wrote chalk wrap
Anna __wrote__ her name with white __chalk__

5. knot rhino knock
A __rhino__ can __knock__ down a tree!

Dictation
Does a ghost need a comb?

© Evan-Moor Corp. • EMC 2789 • Daily Phonics   **Skill:** Reading words with silent letters   93

Listen for It — Day 1

Focus The vowel pairs ai and ay are digraphs that have the long a sound. The vowels ai usually come in the **middle** of a word. The vowels ay usually come at the end of a word.

long a
tail tray

Say the picture name. Read the word.
Then underline the two letters that stand for the **long a** sound.

1. nail 2. hay 3. rain
4. mail 5. clay 6. brain
7. snail 8. paid 9. X-ray

Dictation
1. clay   2. brain   3. snail

© Evan-Moor Corp. • EMC 2789 • Daily Phonics   **Skill:** Identifying long a digraphs   95

Write It — Day 2

Letter Box
ai ay

Say the picture name.
Then write the letters that spell the word.

1. t_ai_l 2. cl_ay_ 3. r_ai_n
4. tr_ai_n 5. n_ai_l 6. sn_ai_l
7. j_ay_ 8. p_ai_nt 9. subw_ay_
10. m_ai_l 11. ch_ai_n 12. br_ai_d

Dictation
1. nail   2. sway   3. pain

96   **Skill:** Identifying long a digraphs   Daily Phonics • EMC 2789 • © Evan-Moor Corp.

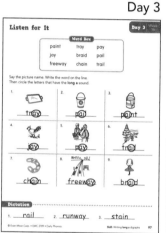

Listen for It — Day 3

Word Box
paint tray pay
jay braid pail
freeway chain trail

Say the picture name. Write the word on the line.
Then circle the letters that have the **long a** sound.

1. tray 2. pail 3. paint
4. jay 5. pay 6. trail
7. chain 8. freeway 9. braid

Dictation
1. rail   2. runway   3. stain

© Evan-Moor Corp. • EMC 2789 • Daily Phonics   **Skill:** Writing long a digraphs   97

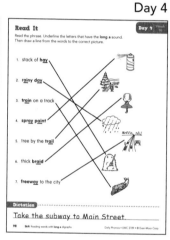

Read It — Day 4

Read the phrase. Underline the letters that have the **long a** sound.
Then draw a line from the words to the correct picture.

1. stack of **hay**
2. rainy **day**
3. **train** on a track
4. spray **paint**
5. tree by the **trail**
6. thick **braid**
7. **freeway** to the city

Dictation
Take the subway to Main Street.

98   **Skill:** Reading words with long a digraphs   Daily Phonics • EMC 2789 • © Evan-Moor Corp.

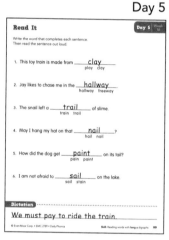

Read It — Day 5

Write the word that completes each sentence.
Then read the sentence out loud.

1. This toy train is made from __clay__
   play clay
2. Jay likes to chase me in the __hallway__
   hallway freeway
3. The snail left a __trail__ of slime.
   train trail
4. May I hang my hat on that __nail__?
   hail nail
5. How did the dog get __paint__ on its tail?
   pain paint
6. I am not afraid to __sail__ on the lake.
   sail stain

Dictation
We must pay to ride the train.

© Evan-Moor Corp. • EMC 2789 • Daily Phonics   **Skill:** Reading words with long a digraphs   99

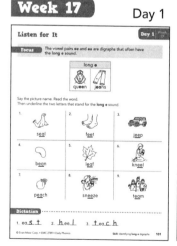

Week 17   Day 1

Listen for It — Day 1

Focus The vowel pairs ee and ea are digraphs that often have the long e sound.

long e
queen jeans

Say the picture name. Read the word.
Then underline the two letters that stand for the **long e** sound.

1. seal 2. feet 3. jeep
4. bean 5. leaf 6. kneel
7. peach 8. sneeze 9. team

Dictation
1. eat   2. heel   3. teach

© Evan-Moor Corp. • EMC 2789 • Daily Phonics   **Skill:** Identifying long e digraphs   101

Listen for It — Day 2

Focus The vowel pairs ey and ie are digraphs that often have the long e sound. The digraph ey usually comes at the end of a word. The digraph ie usually comes in the middle of a word.

long e
joey chief

Say the picture name. Read the word.
Then underline the two letters that stand for the **long e** sound.

1. key 2. donkey 3. thief
4. money 5. field 6. monkey
7. honey 8. piece 9. shield

Dictation
1. brief   2. key   3. grief

102   **Skill:** Identifying long e digraphs   Daily Phonics • EMC 2789 • © Evan-Moor Corp.

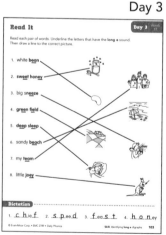

Read It — Day 3

Read each pair of words. Underline the letters that have the **long e** sound.
Then draw a line to the correct picture.

1. white **bean**
2. sweet **honey**
3. big **sneeze**
4. green **field**
5. deep **sleep**
6. sandy **beach**
7. my **team**
8. little **joey**

Dictation
1. chief   2. speed   3. feast   4. honey

© Evan-Moor Corp. • EMC 2789 • Daily Phonics   **Skill:** Identifying long e digraphs   103

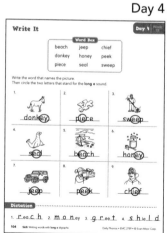

Write It — Day 4

Word Box
beach jeep chief
donkey honey peek
piece seal sweep

Write the word that names the picture.
Then circle the two letters that stand for the **long e** sound.

1. donkey 2. piece 3. sweep
4. seal 5. beach 6. honey
7. jeep 8. peek 9. chief

Dictation
1. reach   2. money   3. greet   4. shield

104   **Skill:** Writing words with long e digraphs   Daily Phonics • EMC 2789 • © Evan-Moor Corp.

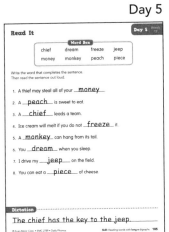
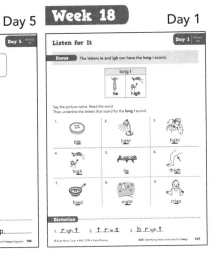

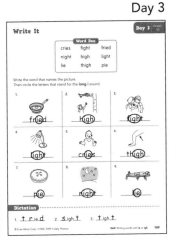

Read It — Day 5

Word Box: chief, dream, freeze, jeep, money, monkey, peach, piece

Write the word that completes the sentence. Then read the sentence out loud.

1. A thief may steal all of your __money__.
2. A __peach__ is sweet to eat.
3. A __chief__ leads a team.
4. Ice cream will melt if you do not __freeze__ it.
5. A __monkey__ can hang from its tail.
6. You __dream__ when you sleep.
7. I drive my __jeep__ on the field.
8. You can eat a __piece__ of cheese.

Dictation: The chief has the key to the jeep.

Listen for It — Day 1

Focus: The letters ie and igh can have the long i sound.

long i: tie, high

Say the picture name. Read the word. Then underline the letters that stand for the long i sound.

1. pie 2. light 3. fight
4. high 5. lie 6. thigh
7. fried 8. night 9. cries

Dictation: 1. right 2. tries 3. bright

Write It — Day 2

Word Box: night, tie, tried, light, fried, thigh, high, pie, bright, lie, cries, right

Read each word. Then write it under ie or igh.

ie	igh
tie	night
tried	light
fried	thigh
pie	high
lie	bright
cries	right

Dictation: 1. dried 2. might 3. fright

Write It — Day 3

Word Box: cries, fight, fried, night, high, light, lie, thigh, pie

Write the word that names the picture. Then circle the letters that stand for the long i sound.

1. fried 2. high 3. fight
4. light 5. cries 6. thigh
7. pie 8. night 9. lie

Dictation: 1. tried 2. sight 3. tight

Read It — Day 4

Say the picture name. Then fill in the circle next to the word that names the picture.

1. ○ fries ● flies
2. ● night ○ tight
3. ● right ○ night
4. ○ tries ● spies
5. ○ dries ● cries
6. ● tights ○ lights
7. ○ thigh ● high
8. ○ tied ○ tried
9. ● bright ○ fright
10. ● lie ○ fie
11. ○ sight ● light
12. ● fried ○ cried

Dictation: 1. cried 2. flies 3. flight

Read It — Day 5

Write the words that complete the sentence. Then read the sentence out loud.

1. bright / light / sight — My desk __light__ is too __bright__.
2. tried / cried / spies — The __spies__ __tried__ to catch the thief.
3. fried / fries / flies — Keep the __flies__ away from my __fries__!
4. right / tie / night — What is the __right__ way to __tie__ a knot?
5. tights / sunlight / cried / dried — I __dried__ my __tights__ in the __sunlight__.

Dictation: I will tie a tight knot.

Listen for It — Day 1

Focus: The vowel pairs oa and oe are digraphs that usually have the long o sound.

long o: toad, doe

Say the picture name. Read the word. Then underline the two vowels that stand for the long o sound.

1. road 2. toe 3. loaf
4. soap 5. hoe 6. foam
7. coach 8. boat 9. toast

Dictation: 1. load 2. foe 3. soak

Listen for It — Day 2

Focus: The letter pair ow is a digraph that can have the long o sound.

long o: crow

Say the picture name. Read the word. Then underline the two letters that stand for the long o sound.

1. mow 2. tow 3. row
4. crow 5. throw 6. window
7. bowl 8. snow 9. grown

Dictation: 1. glow 2. slow 3. blow 4. show

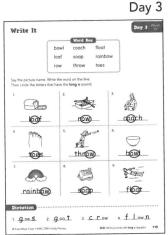
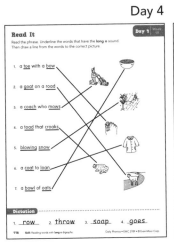
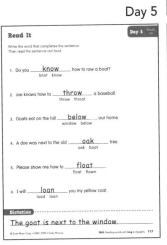

Write It — Day 3

Word Box: bowl, coach, float, loaf, soap, rainbow, row, throw, toes

Say the picture name. Write the word on the line. Then circle the letters that have the long o sound.

1. loaf 2. row 3. coach
4. toes 5. throw 6. bowl
7. rainbow 8. soap 9. float

Dictation: 1. goes 2. goat 3. crow 4. flown

Read It — Day 4

Read the phrase. Underline the words that have the long o sound. Then draw a line from the words to the correct picture.

1. a toe with a bow
2. a goat on a road
3. a coach who mows
4. a toad that croaks
5. blowing snow
6. a coat to loan
7. a bowl of oats

Dictation: 1. row 2. throw 3. soap 4. goes

Read It — Day 5

Write the word that completes the sentence. Then read the sentence out loud.

1. Do you __know__ how to row a boat? (knot / know)
2. Joe knows how to __throw__ a baseball. (throw / throat)
3. Goats eat on the hill __below__ our home. (window / below)
4. A doe was next to the old __oak__ tree. (oak / boat)
5. Please show me how to __float__. (float / flown)
6. I will __loan__ you my yellow coat. (load / loan)

Dictation: The goat is next to the window.

Listen for It — Day 1

Focus: The letter pairs ew and ue are digraphs that usually have the long u sound.

long u: new, clue

Say the picture name. Read the word. Then underline the two letters that stand for the long u sound.

1. fuel 2. flew 3. chew
4. blue 5. grew 6. glue
7. Sue 8. jewel 9. Tuesday

Dictation: 1. news 2. drew 3. true 4. glue

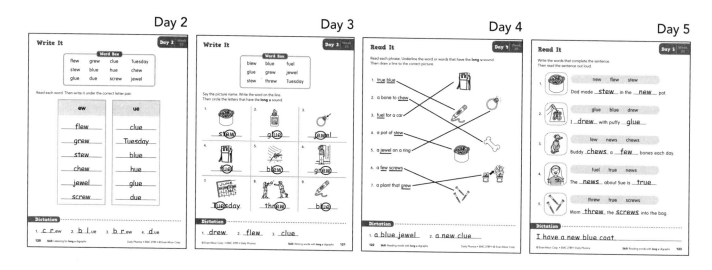

Day 2

Write It — Day 2 Week 20

Word Box
flew   grew   clue   Tuesday
stew   blue   hue   chew
glue   due   screw   jewel

Read each word. Then write it under the correct letter pair.

ew	ue
flew	clue
grew	Tuesday
stew	blue
chew	hue
jewel	glue
screw	due

Dictation
1. c r ew   2. b l ue   3. b r ew   4. d ue

120   Skill: Listening for long u digraphs   Daily Phonics • EMC 2789 • © Evan-Moor Corp.

Day 3

Write It — Day 3 Week 20

Word Box
blew   blue   fuel
glue   grew   jewel
stew   threw   Tuesday

Say the picture name. Write the word on the line.
Then circle the letters that have the long u sound.

1. st ew   2. gl ue   3. j ew el
4. f ue l   5. bl ew   6. gr ew
7. T ue sday   8. thr ew   9. bl ue

Dictation
1. drew   2. flew   3. clue

© Evan-Moor Corp. • EMC 2789 • Daily Phonics   121

Day 4

Read It — Day 4 Week 20

Read each phrase. Underline the word or words that have the long u sound. Then draw a line to the correct picture.

1. true blue
2. a bone to chew
3. fuel for a car
4. a pot of stew
5. a jewel on a ring
6. a few screws
7. a plant that grew

Dictation
1. a blue jewel   2. a new clue

122   Skill: Reading words with long u digraphs   Daily Phonics • EMC 2789 • © Evan-Moor Corp.

Day 5

Read It — Day 5 Week 20

Write the words that complete the sentence.
Then read the sentence out loud.

1. new   flew   stew
   Dad made __stew__ in the __new__ pot.
2. glue   blue   drew
   I __drew__ with puffy __glue__.
3. few   news   chews
   Buddy __chews__ a __few__ bones each day.
4. fuel   true   news
   The __news__ about Sue is __true__.
5. threw   true   screws
   Mom __threw__ the __screws__ into the bag.

Dictation
I have a new blue coat.

© Evan-Moor Corp. • EMC 2789 • Daily Phonics   Skill: Reading words with long u digraphs   123

Week 21

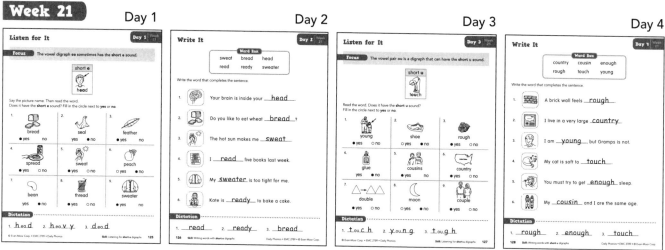

Day 1

Listen for It — Day 1 Week 21

Focus   The vowel digraph ea sometimes has the short e sound.

short e
head

Say the picture name. Then read the word.
Does it have the short e sound? Fill in the circle next to yes or no.

1. bread — yes • no
2. seal — yes • no
3. feather — yes • no
4. spread — yes • no
5. sweat — yes • no
6. peach — yes • no
7. bean — yes • no
8. thread — yes • no
9. sweater — yes • no

Dictation
1. head   2. heavy   3. dead

© Evan-Moor Corp. • EMC 2789 • Daily Phonics   Skill: Listening for short e digraphs   125

Day 2

Write It — Day 2 Week 21

Word Box
sweat   bread   head
read   ready   sweater

Write the word that completes the sentence.

1. Your brain is inside your __head__.
2. Do you like to eat wheat __bread__?
3. The hot sun makes me __sweat__.
4. I __read__ five books last week.
5. My __sweater__ is too tight for me.
6. Kate is __ready__ to bake a cake.

Dictation
1. read   2. ready   3. bread

126   Skill: Writing words with short e digraphs   Daily Phonics • EMC 2789 • © Evan-Moor Corp.

Day 3

Listen for It — Day 3 Week 21

Focus   The vowel pair ou is a digraph that can have the short u sound.

short u
touch

Read the word. Does it have the short u sound?
Fill in the circle next to yes or no.

1. young — yes • no
2. shoe — yes • no
3. rough — yes • no
4. glue — yes • no
5. cousins — yes • no
6. country — yes • no
7. double — yes • no
8. moon — yes • no
9. couple — yes • no

Dictation
1. touch   2. young   3. tough

© Evan-Moor Corp. • EMC 2789 • Daily Phonics   Skill: Listening for short u digraphs   127

Day 4

Write It — Day 4 Week 21

Word Box
country   cousin   enough
rough   touch   young

Write the word that completes the sentence.

1. A brick wall feels __rough__.
2. I live in a very large __country__.
3. I am __young__, but Gramps is not.
4. My cat is soft to __touch__.
5. You must try to get __enough__ sleep.
6. My __cousin__ and I are the same age.

Dictation
1. rough   2. enough   3. touch

128   Skill: Writing words with short u digraphs   Daily Phonics • EMC 2789 • © Evan-Moor Corp.

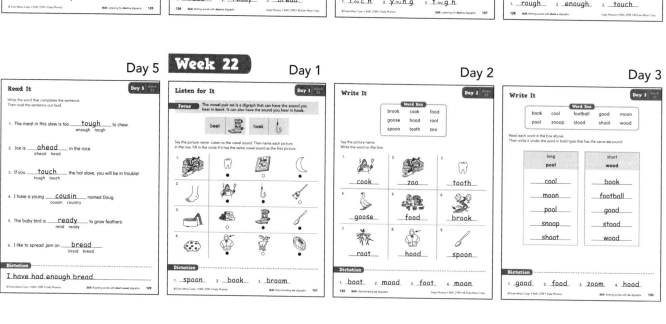

Day 5

Read It — Day 5 Week 21

Write the word that completes the sentence.
Then read the sentence out loud.

1. The meat in this stew is too __tough__ to chew.
   enough   tough
2. Joe is __ahead__ in the race.
   ahead   head
3. If you __touch__ the hot stove, you will be in trouble!
   tough   touch
4. I have a young __cousin__ named Doug.
   cousin   country
5. The baby bird is __ready__ to grow feathers.
   read   ready
6. I like to spread jam on __bread__.
   braid   bread

Dictation
I have had enough bread.

© Evan-Moor Corp. • EMC 2789 • Daily Phonics   Skill: Reading words with short vowel digraphs   129

Week 22

Day 1

Listen for It — Day 1 Week 22

Focus   The vowel pair oo is a digraph that can have the sound you hear in boot. It can also have the sound you hear in hook.

boot   hook

Say the picture name. Listen to the vowel sound. Then name each picture in the row. Fill in the circle if it has the same vowel sound as the first picture.

1.
2.
3.
4.

Dictation
1. spoon   2. book   3. broom

© Evan-Moor Corp. • EMC 2789 • Daily Phonics   Skill: Discriminating oo digraphs   131

Day 2

Write It — Day 2 Week 22

Word Box
brook   cook   food
goose   hood   root
spoon   tooth   zoo

Say the picture name.
Write the word on the line.

1. cook   2. zoo   3. tooth
4. goose   5. food   6. brook
7. root   8. hood   9. spoon

Dictation
1. boot   2. mood   3. foot   4. moon

132   Skill: Discriminating oo digraphs   Daily Phonics • EMC 2789 • © Evan-Moor Corp.

Day 3

Write It — Day 3 Week 22

Word Box
book   cool   football   good   moon
pool   snoop   stood   shoot   wood

Read each word in the box above.
Then write it under the word in bold type that has the same oo sound.

long — pool	short — wood
cool	book
moon	football
pool	good
snoop	stood
shoot	wood

Dictation
1. good   2. food   3. zoom   4. hood

© Evan-Moor Corp. • EMC 2789 • Daily Phonics   Skill: Writing words with oo digraphs   133

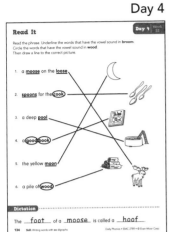 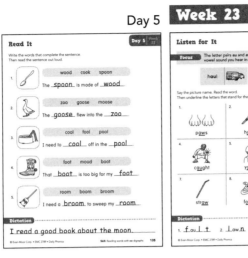  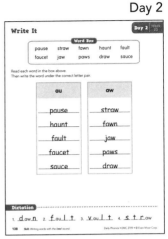

Day 3   Day 4   Day 5   **Week 24**   Day 1

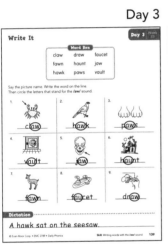 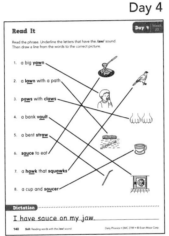 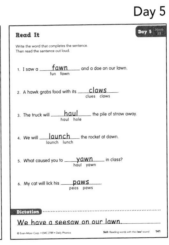 

Day 2   Day 3   Day 4   Day 5

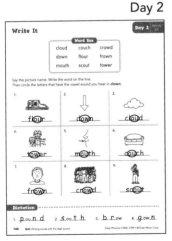   

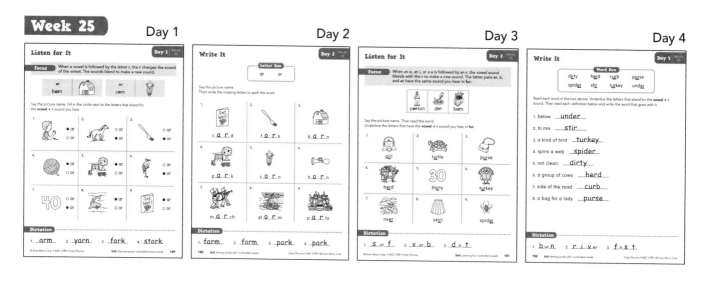

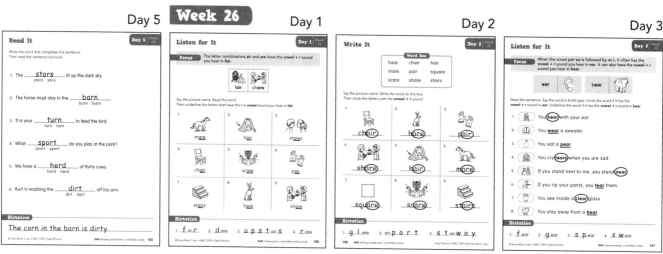

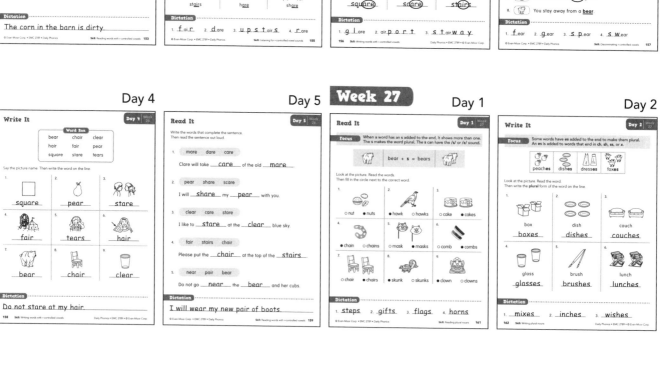

Day 3   Day 4   Day 5   **Week 28**   Day 1

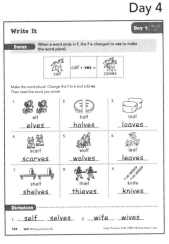

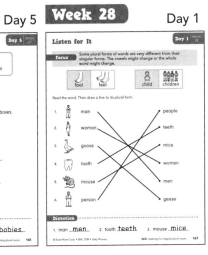

Write It — Day 3

Focus: When a word ends in a consonant and a y, the y is changed to ies to make the word plural. The letter s has the /z/ sound.

fly | fly + ies = flies | flies

Make the word plural. Change the y to ies.
Then read the word you wrote.

1. spy — spies	2. pony — ponies	3. berry — berries
4. candy — candies	5. cherry — cherries	6. penny — pennies
7. puppy — puppies	8. lady — ladies	9. fry — fries

Dictation
1. sky — skies   2. story — stories

163

Write It — Day 4

Focus: When a word ends in f, the f is changed to ves to make the word plural.

calf | calf + ves = | calves

Make the word plural. Change the f to v and add es.
Then read the word you wrote.

1. elf — elves	2. half — halves	3. loaf — loaves
4. scarf — scarves	5. wolf — wolves	6. leaf — leaves
7. shelf — shelves	8. thief — thieves	9. knife — knives

Dictation
1. self — selves   2. wife — wives

164

Read It — Day 5

Word Box
cookies   foxes   dishes   flies
peaches   scarves   spies   kisses

Write the word that completes the sentence.
Then read the sentence out loud.

1. The __spies__ wore dark glasses.
2. Our new set of cups and __dishes__ came in big boxes.
3. Wolves and __foxes__ have bushy tails.
4. Big black __flies__ buzzed around the ponies.
5. Cherries, plums, and __peaches__ have pits.
6. Mom gave the babies many hugs and __kisses__.
7. I will bake two batches of yummy __cookies__.
8. The ladies have new red dresses and __scarves__.

Dictation
The elves made dresses for the babies.

165

Listen for It — Day 1

Focus: Some plural forms of words are very different from their singular forms. The vowels might change or the whole word might change.

foot | feet   child | children

Read the word. Then draw a line to its plural form.

1. man — people
2. woman — teeth
3. goose — mice
4. tooth — women
5. mouse — men
6. person — geese

Dictation
1. man — __men__   2. tooth — __teeth__   3. mouse — __mice__

167

Day 2   Day 3   Day 4   Day 5

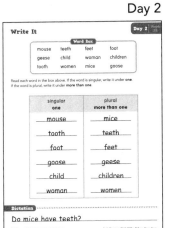

Write It — Day 2

Word Box
mouse   teeth   feet   foot
geese   child   woman   children
tooth   women   mice   goose

Read each word in the box above. If the word is singular, write it under one.
If the word is plural, write it under more than one.

singular one	plural more than one
mouse	mice
tooth	teeth
foot	feet
goose	geese
child	children
woman	women

Dictation
Do mice have teeth?

168

Write It — Day 3

Focus: Some words have the same singular and plural forms. The spellings do not change.

deer | deer   jeans | jeans

The words in bold type have the same singular and plural forms.
Write the plural form of the word on the line.

1. one sheep — a flock of sheep
2. black pants — two pairs of pants
3. a moose — three moose
4. one deer — many deer
5. my glasses — some cute glasses
6. a pair of shorts — two pairs of shorts

Dictation
1. deer   2. jeans   3. sheep   4. shorts

169

Write It — Day 4

Read the first pair of words in each row. Then write the plural form of the word that appears in bold type.

1. one mouse — many __mice__
2. my shorts — these __shorts__
3. a man — a group of __men__
4. your foot — your __feet__
5. a deer — a herd of __deer__
6. one tooth — many __teeth__
7. one child — four __children__

Dictation
The children saw some geese.

170

Read It — Day 5

Write the word that completes the sentence.
Then read the sentence out loud.

1. Some of the __men__ (man men) wore sunglasses.
2. Geese do not have __teeth__ (tooth teeth).
3. Five deer ran past three __moose__ (moose meese).
4. All the __people__ (person people) fled when they saw the mice.
5. These socks are too big for my __feet__ (foot feet).
6. Many __women__ (women woman) tried on jeans at the store.

Dictation
The people saw many sheep on the hill.

171

Week 29   Day 1   Day 2   Day 3   Day 4

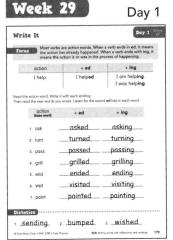
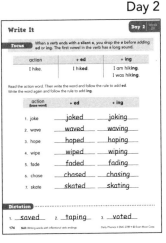
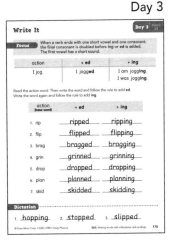

Write It — Day 1

Focus: Most verbs are action words. When a verb ends in ed, it means the action has already happened. When a verb ends with ing, it means the action is or was in the process of happening.

action	+ ed	+ ing
I help.	I helped.	I am helping. I was helping.

Read the action word. Write it with each ending.
Then read the new words you wrote. Listen for the sound ed has in each word.

action (base word)	+ ed	+ ing
1. ask	asked	asking
2. turn	turned	turning
3. pass	passed	passing
4. grill	grilled	grilling
5. end	ended	ending
6. visit	visited	visiting
7. paint	painted	painting

Dictation
1. sending   2. bumped   3. wished

173

Write It — Day 2

Focus: When a verb ends with a silent e, you drop the e before adding ed or ing. The first vowel in the verb has a long sound.

action	+ ed	+ ing
I hike.	I hiked.	I am hiking. I was hiking.

Read the action word. Then write the word and follow the rule to add ed.
Write the word again and follow the rule to add ing.

action (base word)	+ ed	+ ing
1. joke	joked	joking
2. wave	waved	waving
3. hope	hoped	hoping
4. wipe	wiped	wiping
5. fade	faded	fading
6. chase	chased	chasing
7. skate	skated	skating

Dictation
1. saved   2. taping   3. voted

174

Write It — Day 3

Focus: When a verb ends with one short vowel and one consonant, the final consonant is doubled before ing or ed is added. The first vowel has a short sound.

action	+ ed	+ ing
I jog.	I jogged.	I am jogging. I was jogging.

Read the action word. Then write the word and follow the rule to add ed.
Write the word again and follow the rule to add ing.

action (base word)	+ ed	+ ing
1. rip	ripped	ripping
2. flip	flipped	flipping
3. brag	bragged	bragging
4. grin	grinned	grinning
5. drop	dropped	dropping
6. plan	planned	planning
7. skid	skidded	skidding

Dictation
1. hopping   2. stopped   3. slipped

175

Write It — Day 4

Focus: Sometimes a verb has an s or an es added to it. You add an s when a verb ends in a consonant or a silent e. You add es when a verb ends in ch, sh, ss, or x. The es sounds like /iz/.

grab | grabs   reach | reaches   push | pushes   miss | misses   mix | mixes

Read the word. Then write the word and follow the rule to add s or es.
Read the new word you wrote.

1. toss — tosses	2. fix — fixes	3. wash — washes
4. jump — jumps	5. itch — itches	6. pass — passes
7. rush — rushes	8. drop — drops	9. watch — watches

Dictation
1. wishes   2. mixes   3. drips

176

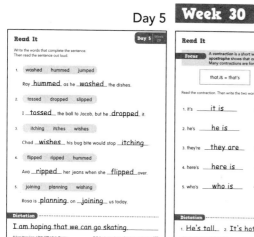

Day 5 — Read It (Week 29)

Write the words that complete the sentence. Then read the sentence out loud.

1. washed   hummed   jumped
   Ray __hummed__ as he __washed__ the dishes.

2. tossed   dropped   slipped
   I __tossed__ the ball to Jacob, but he __dropped__ it.

3. itching   itches   wishes
   Chad __wishes__ his bug bite would stop __itching__.

4. flipped   ripped   hummed
   Ava __ripped__ her jeans when she __flipped__ over.

5. joining   planning   wishing
   Rosa is __planning__ on __joining__ us today.

Dictation
1. I am hoping that we can go skating.

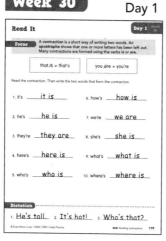

Day 1 — Read It (Week 30)

Focus: A contraction is a short way of writing two words. An apostrophe shows that one or more letters has been left out. Many contractions are formed using the verbs is or are.

that is = that's   you are = you're

Read the contraction. Then write the two words that form the contraction.

1. it's __it is__
2. he's __he is__
3. they're __they are__
4. here's __here is__
5. who's __who is__
6. how's __how is__
7. we're __we are__
8. she's __she is__
9. what's __what is__
10. where's __where is__

Dictation
1. He's tall.   2. It's hot!   3. Who's that?

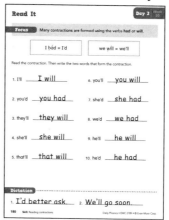

Day 2 — Read It (Week 30)

Focus: Many contractions are formed using the verbs had or will.

I had = I'd   we will = we'll

Read the contraction. Then write the two words that form the contraction.

1. I'll __I will__
2. you'd __you had__
3. they'll __they will__
4. she'll __she will__
5. that'll __that will__
6. you'll __you will__
7. she'd __she had__
8. we'd __we had__
9. he'll __he will__
10. he'd __he had__

Dictation
1. I'd better ask.   2. We'll go soon.

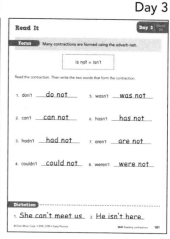

Day 3 — Read It (Week 30)

Focus: Many contractions are formed using the adverb not.

is not = isn't

Read the contraction. Then write the two words that form the contraction.

1. don't __do not__
2. can't __can not__
3. hadn't __had not__
4. couldn't __could not__
5. wasn't __was not__
6. hasn't __has not__
7. aren't __are not__
8. weren't __were not__

Dictation
1. She can't meet us.   2. He isn't here.

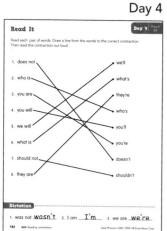

Day 4 — Read It (Week 30)

Read each pair of words. Draw a line from the words to the correct contraction. Then read the contraction out loud.

1. does not
2. who is
3. you are
4. you will
5. we will
6. what is
7. should not
8. they are

we'll / what's / they're / who's / you'll / you're / doesn't / shouldn't

Dictation
1. was not __wasn't__   2. I am __I'm__   3. we are __we're__

Day 5 — Write It (Week 30)

Write the contraction for each pair of words. Then read the sentence out loud.

1. Emma __doesn't__ (does not) know that it's raining.
2. We'll ask Mom if __she'll__ (she will) bake cookies.
3. __What's__ (what is) the reason he's late for the game?
4. I'm sure that this __isn't__ (is not) the right street.
5. I've washed the car, but __you've__ (you have) done nothing.
6. She's saying that we __can't__ (can not) go with you.

Dictation
1. Don't cry.   2. Dad hasn't called me.

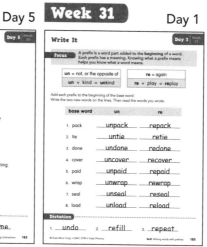

Day 1 — Write It (Week 31)

Focus: A prefix is a word part added to the beginning of a word. Each prefix has a meaning. Knowing what a prefix means helps you know what a word means.

un = not, or the opposite of   re = again
un + kind = unkind   re + play = replay

Add each prefix to the beginning of the base word. Write the two new words on the lines. Then read the words you wrote.

base word	un	re
1. pack	unpack	repack
2. tie	untie	retie
3. done	undone	redone
4. cover	uncover	recover
5. paid	unpaid	repaid
6. wrap	unwrap	rewrap
7. seal	unseal	reseal
8. load	unload	reload

Dictation
1. undo   2. refill   3. repeat

Day 2 — Write It (Week 31)

Focus: Each prefix has a meaning. Knowing what a prefix means helps you know what a word means.

dis = not   re = again   un = not, or the opposite of

Read the word in bold type. Underline the prefix. Then complete the meaning of the word.

1. rerun — to __run__ again
2. uneven — not __even__
3. dislike — to not __like__
4. disallow — to not __allow__
5. refill — to __fill__ again
6. unkind — not __kind__
7. unsure — not __sure__
8. rewrite — to __write__ again
9. disagree — to not __agree__

Dictation
1. repack   2. unzip   3. discover

Day 3 — Write It (Week 31)

dis = not   re = again   un = not, or the opposite of

Read the definition. Write the correct prefix in front of the base word. Then write the new word.

1. not even — __un__even — __uneven__
2. to read again — __re__read — __reread__
3. to paint again — __re__paint — __repaint__
4. not happy — __un__happy — __unhappy__
5. to not agree — __dis__agree — __disagree__
6. not sure — __un__sure — __unsure__
7. to not trust — __dis__trust — __distrust__
8. to count again — __re__count — __recount__

Dictation
1. I will unlock the door.

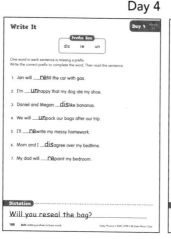

Day 4 — Write It (Week 31)

Prefix Box
dis   re   un

One word in each sentence is missing a prefix. Write the correct prefix to complete the word. Then read the sentence.

1. Jan will __re__fill the car with gas.
2. I'm __un__happy that my dog ate my shoe.
3. Daniel and Megan __dis__like bananas.
4. We will __un__pack our bags after our trip.
5. I'll __re__write my messy homework.
6. Mom and I __dis__agree over my bedtime.
7. My dad will __re__paint my bedroom.

Dictation
1. Will you reseal the bag?

Day 5 — Read It (Week 31)

Write the word that completes the sentence. Then read the sentence out loud.

1. I helped Dad __unload__ (unload unseal) the bags from the car.
2. I __dislike__ (distrust dislike) eating cold pizza.
3. Let's __reheat__ (remove reheat) the leftover pizza for lunch.
4. Chen will __retell__ (retell rewash) the story a second time.
5. That water is __unclean__ (unload unclean) so don't drink it.
6. I __disagree__ (dislike disagree) with your answer.

Dictation
1. I want to reread the book.

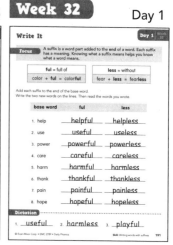

Day 1 — Write It (Week 32)

Focus: A suffix is a word part added to the end of a word. Each suffix has a meaning. Knowing what a suffix means helps you know what a word means.

ful = full of   less = without
color + ful = colorful   fear + less = fearless

Add each suffix to the end of the base word. Write the two new words on the lines. Then read the words you wrote.

base word	ful	less
1. help	helpful	helpless
2. use	useful	useless
3. power	powerful	powerless
4. care	careful	careless
5. harm	harmful	harmless
6. thank	thankful	thankless
7. pain	painful	painless
8. hope	hopeful	hopeless

Dictation
1. useful   2. harmless   3. playful